Nice

Nice
Collected Poems

David Melnick

Edited by

Alison Fraser
Benjamin Friedlander
Jeffrey Jullich
& Ron Silliman

Nightboat Books
New York

Copyright © 2023 by the estate of David Melnick

Introduction and editing Copyright © 2023
by Alison Fraser, Benjamin Friedlander, Jeffrey Jullich,
and Ron Silliman

ISBN: 978-1-64362-157-9

Cover: Detail from *The Vergilius Romanus*, Folio 44 verso, 5th Century.
Collection of Biblioteca Apostolica, Vatican City. Codex Vaticanus Latinus 3867.

Photographs of David Melnick (aka Nice) by David Greene.
Reprinted with permission of the artist.

Frontispiece: "Nice, with glitter lips, rhinestone necklace, pink flamingo,
and Bruno Walter" in Berkeley, 1974.

Page xxxiv: David Melnick and David Doyle (right) at "Center of the Universe"
exhibit at Andy's Donuts, San Francisco, 1975.

Page 232: David Doyle (left) and David Melnick in their apartment, San Francisco, 1975.

Design and typesetting by Rissa Hochberger and Kit Schluter
Typeset in Goudy Old Style

Cataloging-in-publication data is available from the Library of Congress

Nightboat Books
New York
www.nightboat.org

CONTENTS

(POETS; EXIST?

*

Noah Ross

I remember the very real rush of first stumbling on a copy of David Melnick's *PCOET*. All books have aura, sense, energy, and the desire to connect. This *PCOET* had a golden hour halo, and a voice calling out for my hands. I think I barely mumbled "mine." Electricity in the form of static rushed through my body, time almost slowed. If there's such a thing as a bibliomancy spirit, this copy was channeling something heavy. Regardless of energy, this book was elusive, hard to come by in print (as was much of Melnick's publication history). I've only seen one or two since, and nothing else from its publisher, G.A.W.K., the Gay Artists and Writers Kollective. There's a certain jolt in coming across hidden queer remnants of history, a certain power of recognition, a brushing up against queer pasts that realigns the body. In a material form (such as this book), these queer remnants continue to exist. Through encounters and engagement, we keep the work alive.

I found Melnick's work after moving to Berkeley, where he lived in the late 1960s and early '70s before moving across the Bay to San Francisco. I had heard tell of his readings of *PCOET*—his "correct" pronunciations, how only a few could remember the exact sounds his private language formed. I had heard of his famous Homer Group, and read how Melnick's voice was infectious among the other "Homersexuals," how his homophonics perversely instigated a kind of Bacchic frenzy. I remember being shown an event flyer from 1974, from the now-defunct Cody's Books, featuring Melnick reading with Telegraph's "Bubble Lady," Julia Vinograd. I would walk past the former Cody's building daily to feel their presences decades after.

Melnick's work created a kind of orbit, tugging me to its center, but the force that propelled my obsession was impossible to see. Was it that Melnick gave language to queer feelings I had known somewhere deep inside me, but had been unable to voice? Was it that his work points to a kind of unspeakability of these very "qquerl" feelings? I am left wondering what kinds of queer feelings we can represent in queer (il)legibilities. Whether Melnick offers us a cipher, a code, a means of reckoning with language and its limits, feeling and the limits of representing those feelings, too.

David Melnick was a gay poet of San Francisco unlike any other gay poet of San Francisco. A poet whose challenges to writing and reading pose multiple questions and a myriad of possibilities as to what poetry can do, how it can function, what we even consider as its parts, what we recognize as language. The very process of reading him is a disruption of the normative constitution of language. It makes one question the very stability of the word, of poetry's building blocks, opening up space around meaning, sound, and feeling. Reading Melnick makes one stumble.

It's like stumbling into the uncanny. To think to know, to be betrayed, or invited into a space where presumption is illusion. Greek sound, English letters. Private words edging against the known, almost familiar still. Like seeing someone who looks so much like someone else, a lover or a friend from years ago, and feeling one's body jerk in recognition and difference. I find my body moving to call out or embrace this social stranger at the same time I realize they are not, as first assumed, a loved one, but someone I don't know. To stumble like to find my body freezing in the almost-embrace. Does this experience, like Melnick's writing, poke a hole in the fabric of knowledge, the social order of language?

In writing this preface, I keep finding myself lost in this fabric, stumbling for holes, entry points. Procrastinating, doing the dishes, calling Spenser. Today Spenser interviewed the artist Jim Isermann, a seminal designer who fits somewhere between the worlds of craft and art. In Spenser's words, he's been "slept on." From three thousand miles away,

Spenser is in my living room tonight via speakerphone, wondering whether camp allows us to "find joy in a failure of representation." I find a camp irony in my own stumbling around this writing, in my attempts to make meaning of a poet who released us from the burden of meaning.

I wonder how Melnick and Isermann reflect one another, these two underappreciated California artists who rest somewhere in the in-between. Gays who don't fit neatly into scenes or easy timelines, canons even. Gays working in forms that might not be read as gay initially. Melnick, a peripheral Language poet taken up by conceptualists, decidedly not New Narrative, not doing what the other queers were doing, but inserting gay affect into otherwise mostly straight-helmed schools of writing.[1] Is this queer disruption?

There is a queer disruption in how Melnick unearths humor, light, loss, a spectrum and a depth of feeling from precision-based language. PCOET's private language, an idiolect seemingly illegible, dances with resonances of potential meaning and emotional valences ("o sordea, o weedsea!"). Blowing through the homophonic translation-cum-queer romp of *Men in Aïda* invites a reader to break out into laughter tinged with ecstasy, a sense of giddiness and joy in the reproduction of epic Greek into "recognizable" "English." Equally, the "DEATH DEATH DEATH DEATH"-filled *A Pin's Fee* and the nearly romantic, lyrical, Genet-esque hustling poems of *Eclogs* cannot help but leak intensities of affect: deep pain, loss, utter loneliness. To quote Ron Silliman's "Melnick's Pin," "The project is, as it has been always, how best to scribe emotion?"[2]

Through wrestling with and bypassing straight meaning, Melnick's atmospheres of affect carry what our language cannot encompass or represent without failure. The space in between meaning hints at emotional realms unspeakable. What is contained in his words and what rests outside of containment? Consider the following "MORALE" from "We Zonked Him Into Being Whorlmless," in *A Pin's Fee*:

Go Climb Into Yourself

fokked / ting

Major pin Gap   prain gap

A LOOSE URN GATHERS NO MOTHS. NO MOTHERS. NO MOSSED.

What do we find when we climb into ourselves? I hear Kevin Killian say, "The tortoise goes back into its shell to gain strength."[2] Is this a climb or a retreat? A process of being both fucked ("fokked") and still unfolding ("ting" or even "fokkedting")? Fucked and fucking? What's evident is the gap, a Major gap. I am inspired to not only read, but sound, see, hear this gap. Inspired to be contained and uncontainable (loose). There is an almost aphoristic sense of a great truth around loss and death, of isolation, a distance (in spaces) from the nuclear family, from chosen family (our queer mothers, our mentors). A language-oriented grappling with the unspeakable losses of the HIV/AIDS epidemic. Meaning is just one gesture, what the loose urn does not gather, an assonance, resonant in building murmurs. What Melnick's vowels occlude is "MISSED." I want to say, "YES MISSED."

There is an almost utopian reading of Melnick's denial, his repeated NO's. What if, since "NOBODY WILL REMEMBER US ANYWAY," we, as queer readers and writers, could somehow be liberated from the constraints of language, of form, of siloed schools, free to use them as our own attachments and personal experiences require? Free to take words and collide them into another sense, another possibility, another sound. Free to create our own codes, our own gay ethics, ones that "still appeal, eh?"

I look around contemporary poetry and see queer writers working through these questions. I see poets inflecting the lineage of Language poetry with queer thinking, perhaps using seemingly anti-subjective, anti-autobiographical forms while foregrounding queer life and practices. I see Kimberly Alidio's : once teeth bones coral : and how its "linguistic queering of intimacies" (from the acknowledgements) works through Language and New Narrative inheritances. Or I think about Caroline Bergvall's work, for its investment in Old and Middle English (Meddle English, Drift, or Alisoun Sings), as much as for Goan Atom, a text where sliding words form new, queer products: "dragging a badl Eg." I wonder whether Cody-Rose Clevidence's deconstruction of nature in Beast Feast and Flung Throne approaches the contemporary eclogue, or stages a departure akin to Melnick's. I check the mail and Ted Rees has sent me a chapbook called Dear Hole. I see, as I see in Melnick, a working-through of gay experience via an investment in language; I picture Ted "wagging / [his] ass" through his Prynne reading group.

My only hope is that these pages inspire future queer readings and writings, and future queer departures. That we take from Melnick not just a vocabulary, but a roadmap toward new construction, routes into qquerl feeling. That Melnick's interventions into legibility inspire our own reckonings with recognition, in various poetic, communal, and political valences—recognition of and by each other, recognition by the state. That our departures, our reckonings, our engagements keep Melnick's voice alive and ensure that this work will continue to exist. What can we learn about how we write queer lives and feelings, in how our writing and our bodies are read, understood, made or unmade legible? In how we engage with the social order of language—to use the terms of camp icon Jack Smith— as Flaming Creatures and not Pasty Normals? And what is contained in Melnick's eventual silence, his late-career reclusion? In his ultimate divestment from writing, publishing, from caring about the institutions of validation? What can we learn about experiencing the void of meaning? What can we learn about commitment?

So, sound him out. Have fun, feel phonemes, imagine possibility. Like complicated selves, these words we see hold more than the meanings we have given them. These sounds we hear hold histories. What you C is not always what you get, what you get not always what you see. To return to Melnick's lyrical beginnings in *Eclogs*, "Why do we mouth" and "Why, now, at the end of his life, a new dimension?" Maybe his own answer:

> when you look for matter you can only begin
> after 'life' has turned it self
> out & framed an area of action apart and
> strange.
> to recapture.

NOTES

1. One example to illustrate this point might be Eileen Myles asking, "Where is the great language poem about AIDS, how could you watch so many people die and not write about it?" in "Yoga for Losers II" published on the Poetry Foundation's website in 2009. Is it time to offer Melnick's *A Pin's Fee* as an answer?

2. Ron Silliman, "Melnick's Pin," https://writing.upenn.edu/epc/authors/melnick/Silliman-on-Melnick.pdf

3. From Kevin Killian's interview with Georgia State University Library on the James Broughton "Big Joy" Collection (March 2011).

INTRODUCTION

*

Alison Fraser, Benjamin Friedlander,
Jeffrey Jullich, and Ron Silliman

The story is probably not true, though one of us heard it from David Melnick himself: after reading Jean-Paul Sartre's *Saint Genet*, he abandoned his dissertation, moved to Paris to be a hustler. The anecdote was shared over the course of an interview in Melnick's apartment in the 1980s and may have been misheard. Or misunderstood, a jeu d'esprit taken too seriously. The interview had been Melnick's welcome suggestion and no less welcome was his offer to transcribe the tapes—which he destroyed. Apparently, he wanted to share his past, but not with posterity. The interview's retraction perhaps qualifies our introduction as a breaking of confidence, but we haven't sufficient facts for a dry history, only the stories of friends and the siftings of memory, along with Melnick's own testimony, which is sparing. The story is also too delicious to set aside entirely. Sartre's 600-page study of Genet, a pre-Stonewall artifact, was first published in English in 1963 (the same year as John Rechy's *City of Night*), and known to Melnick by 1966: as a graduate student at the University of Chicago, he proposed a paper on the topic to Hannah Arendt. One can well imagine the book's appeal in that context: the sexual outcast and criminal lent dignity by existential philosophy, their indignity upheld, made beautiful, by Genet's own prose. Three modes of knowledge brought together in a book: queer experience, philosophy, and literature. Could such a synthesis be achieved by Melnick on his own? Not, back then, in academia. Letting go, he taught his last classes in high heels, with glitter in his beard. What came after is the poetry collected here.

As mentioned above, Melnick was sparing in details about his life, at least in print. The closest he came to autobiography is a bio note for *In the American Tree* (1986), a large anthology of Language writing and the principal context in which his work has heretofore been met. The note includes a memorable self-description, written in the third person:

> This poet's politics are left, his sexual orientation gay, his family Jewish. He has wandered much, e.g., to France, Greece and Spain (whence his mother's ancestors emigrated in 1492). As of this writing, he has never held a job longer than a year-and-a-half at a stretch. He is short, fat, and resembles Modeste Moussorgsky in face and Gertrude Stein in body type and posture.

The combination of Moussorgsky and Stein is telling, since the former, a Russian composer, was Romantic and the latter, a queer icon, avant-garde. Melnick's poetry synthesizes these contrary impulses: rhapsodic yet opaque, a fermentation of experience distilled to form, the work of a math student who fell in love with Shakespeare, wandered much, then found his home in San Francisco—a poet's city, known since the sixties as America's gay capital. These two entwined aspects of the writing—Romantic, avant-garde—are not simply expressions of adult belief; they reach back into his childhood, or so the bio note permits us to suppose. "By the age of 7," we read, "he had invented a private language, and at 13 constructed a semi-private one with a friend." Early on, apparently, he learned the poet's truth: that language holds attractions independent of communication. A lesson duly succeeded by another: that communication, if intimate enough, can retain all the attraction—all the power—of invention. Reading a little into this, one might say that the first lesson made Melnick avant-garde while the second made him Romantic.

We begin with hints, imaginings, and guesses; for these are how we negotiate Melnick's poetry, a body of work that offers up to ear and eye, tongue and mind, what yet withdraws from understanding. But what withdraws can still be followed. With glimpses borrowed from friends and family, the broad outline of Melnick's life can still be traced. He was born in Urbana, Illinois, in 1938, the middle of three brothers. Both parents were first generation, coming to the US in childhood: his mother from Istanbul, his father from Lüblin. During the war, his father was in the army, stationed on the west coast, and the family resettled in Los Angeles. Growing up there, Melnick's passion was music, especially opera, and he himself was an excellent violinist. The summer after high school (finished in Ann Arbor, the family having moved again) he attended Interlochen and was named concertmaster of the orchestra. His younger brother, Daniel, remembers the household as turbulent; Melnick, in retreat, referred to their father (a research pathologist) as "Dr. Melnick." He spent his childhood focused on music and school, and was, perhaps, lonely, though given to passionate attachments, as in the one that yielded his semiprivate tongue: the language of "Meldmonia," a nation formed from its two creators' last names.

His later education was split between the University of Chicago, where he enrolled in 1955, and the University of California, Berkeley, where he completed his undergraduate degree a decade later. Several trips to Europe intervened, including a yearlong stay in Paris at twenty-one, a voyage paid for by selling his violin—a Guarneri given by his father. At Berkeley, he became involved in the Free Speech Movement. Arrested at the sit-ins, he was one of eleven who chose jail while appealing the fine, rejecting bail stipulations as a muzzle on further protest. His involvement in the movement, he later recalled, kept him from attending the Berkeley Poetry Conference, held over the same summer as the appeals (1965). All this time he had been working toward a math degree. A late Shakespeare class altered this direction. He began taking graduate courses in literature, then won a prestigious Wilson Fellowship, which allowed him to return to Chicago for an MA in English. John Taggart was a classmate there—an early and important friendship in poetry. After another stay in Paris, he circled back to Berkeley, now for doctoral work, eventually settling on Shakespeare and modernist poetry for his dissertation. It was probably at this time that his own literary activities became serious. He formed friendships with Ron Silliman and David McAleavey, took creative writing with Denise Levertov, and became involved with *Occident*, the school's literary journal (Robert Duncan published there in the thirties and Diane

Wakoski was an editor in the fifties). In 1970, with Silliman, he assembled a feature for *Chicago Review*, "Fifteen Young Poets of the San Francisco Bay Area" (among the fifteen: David Bromige, Kenneth Irby, Joanne Kyger, George Stanley, and Al Young). In the meantime, according to his brother, two upsetting incidents disenchanted Melnick with academia: the lukewarm response to his dissertation prospectus—an attempt to integrate Renaissance scholarship with his own emerging poetics—and the English Department's denial of tenure to a gay professor. He would abandon the PhD in 1974.

While a graduate student at Berkeley, Melnick kept up a correspondence with Taggart, whose journal *Maps* would publish the only portions of the dissertation to see light: a short essay on Charles Olson and Shakespeare (issue no. 4, 1971) and a longer one on Louis Zukofsky's *Bottom: on Shakespeare* (no. 5, 1973). In one of the letters, Melnick offered Taggart a charming summary of his activities and growth since Chicago:

What's happened to me : is :

1967—(from April) in France plus one month on a Spanish isle. Paris hotel had always been my oasis. Halfway through (in August) I had no money, got a job w/the Herald Tribune as a librarian, then copy-boy! (no art-crit available a la Ashbery for this boy!). Found myself working 72 hrs/wk for $150/mo., so finally (December) quit, received once again into parents' bosom (1st 2 months of 68), started working half-time as a computer (operator) & began school again here.

1968—slowly determining myself in terms of 'poet'; my SARTRISM still strong but wearing off; still wary & reluctant (still am) to take on the baggage (anthropology, occult, etc.) that seemed to possess anyone here who was able to read Duncan & Olson, whom I began looking at seriously now (I remember just not BELIEVING much of it before, as when you pointed me toward stuff in 65, e.g., that Massachusetts acct. books or property records could be 'poetry'; or that Duncan could be serious in an essay talking about GOD). Now living in a furnished room near campus, still reading Renaissance lit. for school.

1969—took (1st & last) course in 'writing' from Levertov, who, it turned out, couldn't read my stuff, so fiasco. I was going to make a clean break w/Renaissance by writing a seminar paper (yes!) on Maximus, then quit altogether; but I retreated, decided to stay, learn Latin.

1969-70—now find myself w/ fellowship & plugged into the degree business. The paper ended up being on Shakespeare, I started to read Virgil, Ovid. Exams to follow (if money again next year) in Oct. 70, then a 'thesis' (on Sh.?) 70-71.

During the years recounted here, Melnick wrote the poems in his first book, *Eclogs*, with the poems in his second, *PCOET*, springing forth soon after. The fertility of his writing in this period was building toward change. This he announced, if indirectly, in a short statement for *Occident*, "A Peoticz, for Morgan," published in 1974. The piece begins with three quotations (unattributed, but by Ruth Benedict, George Herbert, and Wordsworth, on sound, speech, and emotion). After comes a cryptic poem by Melnick himself:

Wheel
     seen up
a / certain raiser
In! vitamin

CLOWN! INK!
    ILLS!
vita   (m) out.

The first stanza evokes an airplane just after takeoff, wheels retracting, with the pun on "curtain raiser" emphasizing that this is a moment of beginning. The second stanza, taking apart and playing on the earlier word "vitamin," suggests that this beginning involves Melnick himself (the "m" in parentheses, though possibly Morgan Wines, for whom the piece was written). The message, if we are reading this correctly, is emphatic: life ("vita") will take off by being "out." A declaration well-suited to this turning point in Melnick's life—the year he abandoned his PhD and moved from Berkeley to San Francisco; it was also the year he met the love of his life, David Doyle, recently arrived in the Bay Area after graduating from Kenyon College. Friends remember Melnick as being quite open about his sexuality in those years, so this was no coming out of the closet. But out, perhaps, into a more public display of himself, as when he taught his last classes in high heels.

The Melnick who took root in San Francisco was already known to friends as Nice. This was the name with which he introduced himself to David Greene, founder of the Gay Artists and Writers Kollective (or G.A.W.K.), a significant source of support for Melnick's creative expression in the seventies. The group held regular meetings with readings and discussions, and made trips together to the opera and theater. Members included Winston Leyland, editor and publisher of Gay Sunshine Press, and Harmodius in Exile (Anthony Rogers), a poet and activist only now receiving his due as a genderfuck artist—a radical form of self-presentation emerging from drag culture in the seventies. The ambience of these G.A.W.K. meetings is caught by Greene in a recollection of one outing to the shore where shelter was taken in an abandoned structure—an outhouse. "I have an indelible image in my memory of Nice, notwithstanding his girth, wearing glittering platform heels, his rhinestone necklace, and carrying a glass of cabernet, making his way down the steep cliff at Land's End toward the outhouse where we were to have our G.A.W.K. picnic, smiling and laughing the whole way down at the outlandishness of his gesture." For Christopher Lonc, another member of the group, the clothes and makeup, while fun in themselves, were no mere costume. They pointed a way past "the blue/pink dichotomy" of gender, making "visible and experiential the nonsense of clearcut opposites." So Lonc put it in an essay for Gay Sunshine, "Genderfuck and Its Delights" (1974). A photograph of Lonc and his lover Gary accompanied the essay, taken by Greene, whose more extensive documentation of the scene includes the landmark exhibit Shameless (1974) and the later Andy's Donuts, Center of the Universe (1975). Photographs of Nice appeared in each.

Bonds of affection, artistic affiliation, and gay community held the G.A.W.K. group together, but this was not Melnick's sole context for literary activity in those years. His poetry readings in the gay community (sometimes in drag, to overflowing crowds) coincided with participation in other scenes. Most notably, he took part in the collective creation of Language writing. The distinctness of these varied contexts and the ease with which Melnick moved among them were characteristic of his life overall. "Even as a kid," recalls Daniel, "my brother had many identities." In like fashion, he had many communities, each refracting his work in a different way. Publication history tells some of the story. His first book, *Eclogs* (1972), was solicited by David McAleavey, a friend from *Occident* and one of the "Fifteen Young Poets" in his coedited feature for *Chicago Review*. McAleavey went on from Berkeley to Cornell, becoming involved with Baxter Hathaway's Ithaca House press, and this opened a conduit for Melnick, Silliman, and another friend from *Occident*, Rochelle Nameroff. McAleavey's expansion of Hathaway's catalogue (which would come to include other poets associated with Language writing) was entirely in keeping with the press's mission. As Marty Cain observes, Ithaca House maintained a fruitful exchange "between subculture and establishment, individual and institution," a mediation Melnick himself was aspiring to achieve in his dissertation and teaching. Ithaca House also offered Melnick a chance to find readers beyond his immediate circle—a traditional path for poets with literary ambitions, though not one he would follow in the end. After Melnick left graduate school, mediation ceased to be a goal and even extending readership ceased to be a major one. The change can be traced bibliographically. Melnick's second book, *PCOET* (1975), was published by G.A.W.K., one of two titles the Kollective produced (the other was by Harmodius in Exile). Simultaneously, *PCOET* made its way into experimental-poetry circles, largely through the effort of its dedicatee, Ron Silliman. Twenty sections appeared in Silliman's *Tottel's* (issue no. 13, 1975) and two more in a feature Silliman curated for *Alcheringa: Ethnopoetics*, "The Dwelling Place: 9 Poets" (vol. 1, no. 2, 1975). Friendship and subculture defined the book's reach; neither institution nor establishment played a role.

As the title of *Eclogs* begins to indicate, Melnick's first book was a kind of pastoral. *PCOET*, with its unexpected "c" wedged into the word "poet," announces something more avant-garde. This made it a good fit for the emerging project of *L=A=N=G=U=A=G=E* magazine, which featured Melnick in its first issue (1978). The feature began with an appreciation by Silliman (titled "Nice"), then came the first poem in *PCOET* and a statement by Melnick: a synopsis of his work to date ending with a poignant claim—that the world of meaning suffocates and fits us badly. A poetry "sliding and gliding just above language" (a motion that recalls the liftoff in "A Peoticz, for Morgan") offers, if not escape, a glimpse of what escape might find:

> The ECLOGS (1967-70) are transparently derivative poems, tho when I wrote them I would never have allowed so, not in the way I now mean it....
>
> Do you like them? They are terribly romantic, personal. Do you like poems that are impossibly oblique yet turn up clues to the movements of the soul of the poet? Hadn't we got beyond that? I hope so!
>
> I do like the "impossibly" part, even if the "oblique" part supposes some referent relative to which obliquities can be measured. The lines are always taking off, sliding and gliding just above language. Good. Also the cadences.
>
> PCOET was written in May-June 1972...except for #2 which was written in Jan. 1975 entirely from the index of an Ichthyology textbook belonging to my lover, David Doyle.
>
> I doubt that any statement will mediate between PCOET and its audience.... The poems are made of what look like words and phrases but are not. I think these poems look like they should mean something.... At the same time, you know that you can't begin to understand what they mean.
>
> What can such poems do for you? You are a spider strangling in your own web, suffocated by meaning. You ask to be freed by these poems from the intolerable burden of trying to understand. The world of meaning; is it too large for you? too small? It doesn't fit. Too bad. It's no contest. You keep on trying. So do I.

In the seventies and eighties, Language writing manifested on both coasts in scenes of varying size and concentrations of activity, linked above all through publication. The largest community was in the Bay Area, supported by multiple venues for readings and talks and a handful of publishing ventures. One such venture: Lyn Hejinian's Tuumba Press, a letterpress chapbook series producing fifty titles between 1976 and 1984. Melnick's *Men in Aïda, Book One* (1983) is the forty-seventh. Arts organizations provided crucial infrastructure in those years; academic institutions were still peripheral: the Language scene as Melnick engaged it was, like G.A.W.K., a subculture.

Melnick's ties to Language writing were personal as well as intellectual. Rae Armantrout, like Silliman, was a friend from Berkeley days; they met in Denise Levertov's creative writing class. Tom Mandel overlapped with Melnick at the University of Chicago. The two formed a reading group in the 1980s, known affectionately as "the Jew group" (David Sheidlower and Benjamin Friedlander were also members). No surprise that, at a moment of peak hostility against Language writing, Melnick would defend the project by way of these friends. For the San Francisco Chronicle (where he became a copyeditor in 1984), Melnick wrote an omnibus review of Armantrout, Mandel, and Silliman—and also of Beverly Dahlen, not usually counted a Language writer but active in the community. Published the day of Silliman's wedding to Krishna Evans, the review began:

> You might think, in our varied and tolerant San Francisco literary scene, that just about any new circle of writers would find its place without provoking too much controversy. No such luck.
>
> A dozen or more Bay Area poets, along with some others on the East Coast, are writing what has come to be known as "language" poetry. Fans of this new approach consider language-centered writing to be a true avant-garde American art form. Detractors call it a disastrous experiment, unreadable—a specter haunting literature. The present writer, peripherally included in the group, leans unabashedly toward the new work.

What follows are brief characterizations of each poet's project, with sample lines as illustration. The emphasis in each case is existential. The priorities of Language writing as conventionally understood are absent (materiality of the sign, mistrust of the first-person singular, ideology critique). Instead, we're shown four modes of being in the world. Thus Armantrout is "a poet in a vortex. She creates a wind around her, then

moves with sharpened energy across natural and social phenomena."
With Silliman, "It does not take long for this poetry to unbalance you.
In doing so, it suggests how people actually move through their lives." Of
Mandel he writes, "a passage that proposes itself as part of a symbolic or
metaphoric whole begins a poem that ends by stretching things beyond—
just beyond—the breaking point." Dahlen instead yields "a portrait of
continual awakenings into consciousness and farewells to it, of chewings,
tearings and layings-out of seen, remembered, read, despaired-of, aban-
doned phenomena." Grasped or out of reach, experience is the subject.

Despite his involvement in this community, Melnick embarked on
no new poetic projects after composing *PCOET* in 1972, a quiescence
of over a decade that explains his absence from two collections aimed at
broadening the Language group's reach (Charles Bernstein's "Language
Sampler" in the *Paris Review* and Silliman's "Realism: An Anthology of
'Language' Writing" in *Ironwood*, both 1982). Possibly, Melnick was in fact
writing but destroying the finished work—we know this occurred at other
times. More likely, he was content to wait for inspiration—or was simply
content. This last prospect was David Greene's conjecture when asked
about poems that might have been shared at G.A.W.K. meetings. Melnick
and Doyle were especially happy in these years, spending long periods in
Greece (where the lovers first visited in 1978). Perhaps, too, Melnick's not
writing was another way of sliding and gliding above language, taking his
cue from *Leaves of Grass* ("I loafe and invite my soul, / I lean and loafe at
my ease"). Or perhaps his cue came from *Dr. Zhivago*. As Greene recalls:

Nice and I had a similar reaction to a scene from the film *Dr. Zhivago*,
in which the poet, Yuri, Omar Sharif, and his lover Lara, Julie
Christie, are alone together in an idyllic but frozen retreat, enjoying
their happiness and isolation. Lara asks Yuri: "Will you write today?"
Yuri pauses a moment, a contented smile flits across his face, then
he says, "No. I shan't write today." Nice and I would sometimes ban-
ter similarly about what we were up to with one of us saying to the
other: "Will you write today?" to which the other would invariably
and playfully reply: "No. I shan't write today." We shared a sense of
humor about the fickleness of the muse—or perhaps, more prop-
erly, an ability to laugh at the waxing and waning of our creative oom
pah pah—especially when it waned in moments of personal bliss.

Whatever the reason for the pause in writing, it makes piquant a comment recorded in *Writing/Talks*, a collection of lectures by Language writers edited by Bob Perelman, who included transcripts of the discussions that followed. In 1983, Rae Armantrout gave a talk on "Poetic Silence." During the discussion, Melnick said:

> One of the kinds of silence that you talked about was where you don't speak, and there is a great deal of language going on in your head that is waiting to be spoken or not be spoken. And then there is another kind where you think of the whole world of language and find that its horizon might be a total void.

The first kind of silence is a pause or period of waiting in which one's relationship to language remains unchanged. The second is more total, but also, unexpectedly, more desired. As Melnick goes on to note, the void beyond language can sometimes be sensed within it, as in the work of John Ashbery, "especially between the lines of a poem like 'Europe.'" At such moments, the "rush of the world" goes away, one escapes what Melnick in his statement for *L=A=N=G=U=A=G=E* calls "suffocation by meaning." Achieving that escape in poetry, however fleetingly, was worth waiting for. To breathe free is the goal. Short of that, silence is sufficient.

As the seventies gave way to the eighties, the broad field of experimental poetry began to coalesce in new groupings. In the Bay Area, communities associated with Language writing, the Poetics Program at New College, and New Narrative were especially active. Melnick's primary ties were to the first of these, but he also maintained contacts with the second. Through these contacts, he became a member of the Homer Group, an *Iliad* reading group organized by Robert Duncan in 1981, in the second semester of the newly established Poetics Program at New College. At its formation, the group had eight members including Melnick. Two of the members were core faculty at New College: Robert Duncan and Diane Di Prima. The others were David Levi Strauss, Susan Thackrey, Aaron Shurin—with whom Melnick shared the stage in 1975 for "Organ Recital, Gay Poets in Concert"—Steve Anker, and Noel Stack. The weekly meetings continued for six years, joined by such later attendees as Michael McClure, Jim Powell, and David Doyle. Working in five- to twenty-line increments, the group chanted and translated the Greek text, guided by reference books. A few members had prior experience with the language but most learned as they went along. Strauss remembers Melnick and Shurin as "the most melodious rhapsodes." He also recalls Duncan referring to the group "as a *marriage*, that we were married to the poem." Melnick, in a conversation with Gordon Faylor, reported, more amusingly, "We called ourselves the Homersexuals." Through his involvement with the group, Melnick came to type the manuscript of Duncan's *Ground Work: Before the War* (1984). He also conducted and transcribed a late interview with the poet. Rare among the Language writers, he was welcomed into Duncan's fold.

For Melnick, involvement with the group had a further impact—resumption of his own poetry. In a natural extension of the group's approach to Homer's Greek, he undertook a homophonic translation (appropriately enough, he began work while in Greece with Doyle). The end result, his longest and most consequential work, would take its title from the opening words: *Men in Aïda*, Melnick's equivalent for the *Iliad*'s first words, "menin aeide" (literally, "of wrath sing"). As his treatment of this opening already indicates, a homophonic translation attends to the sound of language, not its meaning—an ideal practice for a poet who found meaning suffocating. Unlike transliteration, which merely transcribes the sound (a useful device when the alphabet is unfamiliar, as with Greek), homophonic translation finds words to match the sound. Consider the long opening sentence of Homer's poem in Richmond Lattimore's English version:

> Sing, goddess, the anger of Peleus' son Achilleus
> and its devastation, which put pains thousandfold upon the Achaians,
> hurled in their multitudes to the house of Hades strong souls
> of heroes, but gave their bodies to be the delicate feasting
> of dogs, of all birds, and the will of Zeus was accomplished
> since that time when first there stood in division of conflict
> Atreus' son the lord of men and brilliant Achilleus.

The Greek behind this reads in transliteration:

> Menin aeide thea Peleiadeo Achileos
> oulomenen, he muri Achaiois alge etheke,
> pollas d' iphthimous psuchas Aidi proiapsen

heroon, autous de heloria teuche kunessin
oionoisi te pasi, Dios d' eteleieto boule,
ex hou de ta prota diasteten erisante
Atreides te anax andron kai dios Achilleus.

And Melnick's homophonic version:

> Men in Aïda, they appeal, eh? A day, O Achilles!
> Allow men in, emery Achaians. All gay ethic, eh?
> Paul asked if tea mousse suck, as Aïda, pro, yaps in.
> Here on a Tuesday. 'Hello,' Rhea to cake Eunice in.
> 'Hojo' noisy tap as hideous debt to lay at a bully.
> Ex you, day. Tap wrote a 'D,' a stay. Tenor is Sunday.
> Atreides stain axe and Ron and ideas 'll kill you.

Melnick retains a few of the proper nouns (Achilles, Achaians, Atreides) but otherwise departs from the sense of the original. He also departs from the grammar of the original, replacing Homer's single sentence with twelve short ones, two of them questions. Focusing on sense, Lattimore gives "feasting / of dogs, of all birds" for Homer's "teuche kunessin / oionoisi te pasi." Melnick, focusing on sound, gives "to cake Eunice in. / 'Hojo' noisy tap as," plus the first syllable of "hideous." New proper nouns like "Eunice" repopulate the poem, coexisting with the old. Were it not for this coexistence, one might argue that Melnick had terraformed Homer's world, preparing the way for a new form of life, a different imagination of the social. Instead, he lets the old still be heard, if faintly: two modes of being, each disclosed in the same set of sounds—one ruled by "gay ethic," the other by "wrath."

Melnick may have intended to translate the entirety of the *Iliad* but he determined, finally, that three books would be sufficient. Lyn Hejinian solicited the first for Tuumba Press. Melnick—always diffident about publication—was content to let the others circulate privately. Book II would not appear until 2002, uploaded by Craig Dworkin as part of the Eclipse archive. Book III would not appear until 2014, in a bilingual edition introduced by Sean Gurd (Uitgeverij was the publisher). In the interim, Melnick wrote only one other poem, *A Pin's Fee* (1987), also unpublished until this century, when Jeffrey Jullich brought it out in his online journal *Logopoeia*. Since then it has figured prominently in scholarship on poetry and AIDS. His reasons for eschewing or delaying publication were no doubt varied, but acute self-criticism was part of it. He told Gordon Faylor he stopped writing in the eighties because "I lost interest in my own work," and in sharing *A Pin's Fee* with Jullich he described it as "indistinguishable from thousands of students' writing." With more humility than self-rebuke he told Robert Duncan, "I wish I could say, since I'm so tongue-tied when wanting to write you, that I'd let my own poetry stand as homage, but I know it would take someone with far greater powers than mine—I don't think *that* choir is giving auditions to the likes of me!"

Into the early nineties Melnick continued to attend readings. But these were shattering years for both the gay community and Melnick personally, and as the decade pressed on, he began to withdraw. *A Pin's Fee* shows how overshadowed by death his social imagination had become by the late eighties ("cloven world//*horror mundi*, / ...eclipsed world," reads one passage), though the poem also expresses anguish over fissures in his relationship with Doyle, to whom the book, like *Men in Aïda*, is dedicated. The two sources of pain—breakup and the AIDS crisis—are brought together in the title of one section: "NOBODY WILL REMEMBER US ANYWAY." In another, he summons the will to go on:

NO to hatred. NO to fists. NO to slimy reasons.

NO to the sneer. NO to rage coupled with power.

NO to the sway of the wicked.

But the passage ends deflatingly, "Uh, O.K.," a sign of exhaustion. Doyle's subsequent death from AIDS in 1992 was simply crushing.

With Melnick's later years our narration falters. Work, opera, friendship, and then failing health. Poetry recedes, though young admirers would write or come calling, leading at last to the publication of key texts. Gordon Faylor published his interview on Open Space, SFMOMA's online platform, drawing new readers. Longtime readers—Charles Bernstein and Mark Scroggins among them—continued advocacy. In

2000, Melnick retired as a copyeditor. In 2006, he developed hydrocephalus—water on the brain. Doctors introduced a shunt in the spine to drain it, which didn't help, then proposed a shunt in the brain, which Melnick refused. By 2015 he was bedridden, with friends and family checking in. These were not cheerless years by any means. Melnick became a frequent contributor to opera discussion boards, and David Greene recalls "LOTS of bad (usually gay) movies," adding: "he almost always found something to appreciate—and that something was clearly a thing he was bringing to the experience." In 2020, after a series of emergencies, Melnick moved to an acute care facility. He died on February 15th, 2022, one day before his 84th birthday.

*   *   *   *

In parallel with his life, Melnick's poetry also yields a story, a compact one. Four books comprise his legacy: *Eclogs* (written 1967-1970), *PCOET* (mostly 1972), *Men in Aïda* (1983), and *A Pin's Fee* (1987). As the dates of composition show, his years of creativity span a crucial two decades in the rise of queer community: his first book begun before Stonewall; his last written in the crisis years of AIDS. And each book reflects a truth of its moment, though in a manner entirely its own. In *Eclogs*, the beautiful façade of coded language preserves an experience it screens from view. *PCOET* yields to the joy of invention, creating a language all its own. *Men in Aïda*, the pinnacle of this span, is his epic: an act of gay worldbuilding, embracing the past and transforming it through homophonic translation. *A Pin's Fee*, the shortest of the four, is anguished: its last word, "DEATH," repeating forty-five times. After this, nothing. For the rest of Melnick's life, another thirty-five years, no other poetry would surface.

If one regrets the absence of further work, there is, nonetheless, a beautiful roundness to what we have. This is especially evident when the first and last books are looked at side by side, for *Eclogs* and *A Pin's Fee* bear a family resemblance. Romantic in subject matter, avant-garde in technique, written in discrete, titled sections, with hints of autobiography and snatches of foreign language, they are both, in Melnick's words, "impossibly oblique yet turn up clues to the movements of the soul of the poet." Their differences, of course, are also profound. If *Eclogs* is pastoral,

xxi

A *Pin's Fee* is necropastoral (borrowing a term from Joyelle McSweeney). But despite this difference, they share a grounding: both are adjustments to the world we know. The two books that came between create worlds: *PCOET* by imagining a new language, *Men in Aïda* by reimagining the social.

The ten sections of *Eclogs* are described by Melnick at the start of the poem as "10 times or tenses," which suggests a sequence of discrete epochs in the life of the poet or poem. The experience of reading unfolds a more complicated story. Myth and actuality, literary and personal reference, are intermixed, resulting in a feeling of simultaneity as well as sequence. Despite realistic touches (like the street address of his Paris hotel), Melnick's arcadia is not a fixed location in space or time, but a construct of memory held in language. In this sense, his tenses are not grammatical forms for orienting time but poetic forms for orienting feeling. One is not surprised to learn that he considered calling the poem "Brain-Eclogues."

The book's allusions to the eclogue tradition are many but Melnick pointedly begins his poem in the city, with bus and elevated train—a train that "seeks forwardness," and which, in descending underground, "arouses desire." His poem is pastoral—is concerned with idyllic nature—primarily in what it seeks. His "smooth-shaven Pan . a shoulder ablaze" may be a citation from literature; it may be a sighting from the bus. In either case, it identifies a longing. Like Andre Gide, who named a defense of homosexuality after one of Virgil's shepherds—*Corydon*, a name also appearing in *Eclogs*—Melnick turns to tradition to make the queer natural and the natural queer. As he writes in the second section:

> when you look for matter you can only begin
> after 'life' has turned it self
> out & framed an area of action apart and
> strange

The eclogue as "an area of action" has "life" as its frame, but neither eclogue nor life is the "matter" in this formulation; they only prepare the way for seeking it. Melnick's seeking is often but not exclusively erotic in the poem, though this is guesswork on our part—the poem offers only glimpses of its goal. As he tells us in the title of section three, "*THESE*

ARE THE ASPECTS OF THE PERFECT": aspects, and not the thing itself, because the perfect cannot be grasped by language (though language meets us wherever we turn, a point Melnick himself makes in section eight).

The step from *Eclogs* to *PCOET* was short in time but long in imagination, crossing a deep divide in conceptions of poetic language. For all its private association and cryptic narration, *Eclogs* assumed a shared vocabulary and shared tradition with its reader. *PCOET* shed such assumptions, inviting the reader to confront life without them. *PCOET*'s language is unique to the poem; no dictionary can help us with paraphrase or translation:

33.

seta

colecc

puilse, i

canoe

it spear heieo

as Rea,   cinct pp

pools we sly drosp

Geianto

　　　(o sordea,   o weedsea!)

Of course, we take our bearings from our prior experiences of reading and in this sense *PCOET* is not without tradition. Melnick himself has said he modeled the poems, shape-wise, on the work of Denise Levertov; and he alludes within the poem to James Joyce and Gertrude Stein (section 52: "letr joices // nm Gerrude S̶t̶ sti"). Moreover, here and there, as in the section above, words we do know appear—loanwords, we assume, absorbed into *PCOET*'s fictional language—intimating a history of exchange and translation between cultures. We're enticed into thinking of the poem as interpretable, if not yet by us. Yet even absent a line-by-line understanding, we still try to intuit the purpose of the poem. Or rather purposes, since metafiction is involved. Melnick's intention in creating *PCOET* is not the same, presumably, as that of the author we might imagine for the poem, since the latter was writing for readers who shared *PCOET*'s tongue and Melnick for us, who lack that capacity. But whatever scenario we imagine, however rich in speculation or stripped of understanding, the reader-writer relation remains social. And this social relation as arranged by Melnick *for us* is one in which the rules no longer obtain, in which we draw more than usually on our own resources and desires.

Puzzling over *PCOET*, individual words often stand out, either for evoking other languages (the poem's first word, "thoeisu," appears Greek; the last, "sofka," could be Hebrew), or for edging to the limits of the linguistic altogether ("g;ɫrdled" in section 59, which incorporates a semicolon and superimposes "e" on "l"). Reading with an eye toward how the poem was composed, one finds inspired typos ("psonge" instead of "sponge" in section 3), fragments ("execu" in section 30), and simple alterations of letter ("foretoid" in section 67). Classical rhetoric has a term for such manipulation: metaplasmus. Melnick has "metapoif" (section 11), which may not mean the same thing but does perform it (or rather, *poif*orm it). Performance, indeed, is a useful way to think about this poem. *PCOET* can be sounded if not yet understood, and Melnick himself enjoyed reading the poem in public; it was a mainstay of his G.A.W.K. performances. Occasionally, too, individual words open to understanding in a way that whole sequences cannot, functioning as individual poems in their own right—poems that operate through condensation rather than syntax. In a beautiful reading, Colin Herd brings this perspective to "qquerl," the first word of section 26. "Semantically," he writes, it emanates "queer", "query", "querulous", "quarrel", "queue", "curl", "querk". Maybe the skiing term "quersprung", too, the act of negotiating obstacles through right angled pivots. In other words, it's a semantic bundle of troubling, activating, questioning. Soundedly, too, the double "q" makes for a stutter or glitch, followed by the curl of the "uerl". . . . This is a qquerl-ous text. It's qquerl-ous in its initial illegibility, in its exploration of the materiality of the signifier, and in its poly-legibility.

Melnick encourages us to think in this way by ending with several sections that have a single word as their text (sections 62-65, 67, 69-70, 73-76, and 78-83).

Commentators have noted a precedent for *PCOET* in the sound poetries of Russian Futurism and Dada, though Melnick's inspirations were probably more personal: his training in music, study of mathematics, and childhood invention of a private language. Literary inspiration is more prominent with his next book, *Men in Aïda*, as its method of composition would have been familiar from Celia and Louis Zukofsky's *Catullus*. Comparison of the Zukofskys' text with *Men in Aïda* is instructive, as the differences speak directly to Melnick's aims. Here is the Latin for Catullus 70, a quatrain, with a literal rendering in prose (by Leonard C. Smithers, 1894):

> Nulli se dicit mulier mea nubere malle
> quam mihi, non si se Iuppiter ipse petat.
> dicit: sed mulier cupido quod dicit amanti,
> in vento et rapida scribere oportet aqua.

No one, saith my lady, would she rather wed than myself, not even if Jupiter's self crave her. Thus she saith! but what a woman tells an ardent amourist ought fitly to be graven on the breezes and in running waters.

And the Zukofskys' homophonic translation:

> Newly say dickered my love air my own would marry me all
> whom but me, none see say Jupiter if she petted.
> Dickered: said my love air could be o could dickered a man too
> in wind o wet rapid a scribble reported in water.

This follows the sound closely, as one expects given the method, but it follows the sense too, somewhat, departing from sound at the end to preserve the important word "water" ("aqua"). Not all of the Zukofsky *Catullus* works this well as translation, but the intention to translate is evident throughout in the preservation of proper nouns, as here with "Jupiter." Nor do the Zukofskys add names of their own, as Melnick does. Here are the first four lines of *Men in Aïda*, Book II:

Alloy, men! Rot the 'I,' take Guy and Harry's hippo-core (-rust) tie.
You don't panic? He idea'd Duke an 'aid-'em-us' hoop nose.
A low gay murmur is a cat tap. Prayin' a hose sock 'll lay ya,
Timmy say 'Oh les' see de polyosophy' (new sin: a guy own).

Four names absent from the original are introduced here (Guy, Harry, Duke, and Timmy), while those that do appear in Homer are left out (Achilles, Achaean). Translation is not the point, or even remotely discernible. Melnick's "hoop nose" derives from "hupnos" ("sleep"), and even the Greek-sounding "polyosophy" is pure invention, sprung from "poleas epi" ("many beside"). Here is the full passage in Greek, transliterated, with Richmond Lattimore's translation:

alloi men rha theoi te kai aneres hippokorustai
heudon pannuchioi, Dia d' ouk eche nedumos hupnos,
all' ho ge mermerize kata phrena hos Achilea
timesei, olesei de poleas epi neusin Achaion.

Now the rest of the gods, and men who were lords of chariots,
slept night long, but ease of sleep came not upon Zeus
who was pondering in his heart how he might bring honour
to Achilleus, and destroy many beside the ships of the Achaians.

In place of translation, Melnick creates content of his own, much of it queer, hearing in the Greek "A low gay murmur" drowned out by the *Iliad*'s din of battle (or in this case, by the mere "pondering" ["ge mermerize"] of battle).

Men in Aïda's queer content points to another important difference from *Catullus*: sex. A surprising one given the bawdiness of the Latin original. Its paucity in the Zukofskys' text is not a matter of method; Melnick obeys the same constraint. In Melnick's hands, however, homophonic translation admits sex; with the Zukofskys, it leads to expurgation. Consider the opening of Catullus 16, a poem so filthy its offending words were often left in Latin:

Pedicabo ego vos et irrumabo

Smithers in his nineteenth-century prose version has this:

I will paedicate and irrumate you

—meaning "sodomize" and "face-fuck." The Zukofskys replace profanity with euphemism:

Piping, beaus, I'll go whoosh and I'll rumble you

Likewise, in Catullus 97, where the Latin gives "culus mundior et melior" ("anus cleaner and better"), the Zukofskys arrive at "(cool) hole's moonier and mellower"—a delightful line, but sly where Catullus is explicit. There are exceptions to this softening of the Latin's vulgarity. Catullus 40 has "pervenias in ora vulgi" ("be in the mouth of the crowd"), for which the Zukofskys give "purr in the public vulva." By and large, however, *Men in Aïda*'s explicitness is more Catullus-like than *Catullus*, though not, as with the Latin poet, for the sake of vitriol. Melnick's bawdiness is for its own sake; his poem is orgiastic:

A yea toy, take cock, is too full of fresh men Tuesday
aiei toi ta kak' esti phila phresi manteuesthai (Book I, line 107)
Always the evil things are dear to your heart to prophesy (Lattimore)

Air comb, a cone up any ass, up a cake, a mop, a lame mizzen
erchom echon epi neas, epen kekamo polemizon (Book I, line 168)
yet dear to me go back to my ships when I am weary with fighting
    (Lattimore)

Hullaballoo may own a league, goes many anal in a thorax
alla polu meion: oligos men een linothorex (Book II, line 529)
but far slighter. He was a small man armoured in linen (Lattimore)

Oh spittle do lick yonder penis. Sot up at Rico loathe us
hos pote Doulichiond' apenassato patri cholotheis (Book II, line 629)
who angered with his father had settled Doulichion (Lattimore)

In thee, Moe, my mouth tas' a lick semen alley leasin'.
en thumoi memaotes alexemen alleloisin (Book III, line 9)
stubbornly minded each in his heart to stand by the others (Lattimore)

And there is more, much more: "Ate Timmy's anal. Long are" ("etimesen: helon gar" [Book 1, line 507]), "this tea. All you cop ate ass on" ("th' histia leuka petassan" [Book II, line 480]), "Lou, groan hole, ate Ron" ("lugron olethron" [Book II, line 873]). The cumulative effect of these passages is enhanced by other lines that are less blunt yet still salacious ("car echo moaned as a guy ooze" ["kare komoontas Achaious" {Book II, line 51}]), by direct expression of queer desire ("Hi, homo! / Kurt, oh a piece! Status" ["hoi omo / kurto epi stethos" {Book II, lines 217-18}]), and by nearly two hundred fifty repetitions of the word "gay."

Men in Aïda's relationship to Homer's Greek text is more complex than this array of examples shows, and readers interested in that dimension should seek out Sean Gurd's introduction to the first full printing of the poem in 2014. Persuasively, Gurd argues that Melnick's engagement with the *Iliad* is irreducible to sound alone, and that, as a reader, he was more philologist than translator. Even in the area of sound, notes Gurd, interpretation is required, since the pronunciation of ancient Greek is contested—and Melnick's strategies vary. The correlation of Greek and English by sound is thus not simply a matter of hearing, but "is grounded in a confrontation of phonetic systems." Attending to that confrontation, Gurd sees Melnick's handling of sound as itself a form of cultural analysis. More provocatively, he offers "etymological queering" as an alternative to "homophonic translation." In etymology, sonic similarities between words acquire "explanatory force." Melnick's sonic equivalents are etymologies and not translations, Gurd argues, because they invite new understanding instead of reproducing an old one.

The connection between *Aïda* and *Iliad* cannot be severed, but, looked at in its own capacity as a poem in English, Melnick's text is most notable for its non-Homeric qualities. In this respect, it resembles a precursor quite distinct from *Catullus*: Luis d'Antin van Rooten's homophonic rendering of Mother Goose into French, *Mots d'Heures: Gousses, Rames: The d'Antin Manuscript* (1967), which purports to be a newly discovered medieval text. Supported with explanatory notes in English, a pastiche of scholarship, van Rooten's book inspired two sequels that kept his ingenious structure: Ormonde de Kay's *N'Heures Souris Rames: The Coucy Castle Manuscript* (1980) and John Hulme's *Mörder Guss Reims: The Gustav Leberwurst Manuscript* (1981). What all three works hold in common with *Men in Aïda* is their imagination of a world quite other than the one presented by the source material. For van Rooten, de Kay, and Hulme, that source, the nursery rhyme, is a kind of charm, an abracadabra for conjuring rabbits from hats. For the trick to come off, verbal dexterity—the magician's sleight of hand— is required. Melnick's dexterity is all the more impressive as he foregoes the apparatus they rely on to make their worlds accessible. His we enter purely through sounding. In a winning phrase, Aaron Shurin characterizes that sounding—the music of Melnick's poem—as "a goofball rapture." And this points toward one other resemblance between Melnick's work and that of van Rooten, de Kay, and Hulme: all of their worlds blend the real and ridiculous. We laugh as we read.

There is no laughter in *A Pin's Fee*, which takes its title from a melancholy passage in *Hamlet*. In the first act, the ghost motions the prince to step away from his friends. The friends, alarmed, urge Hamlet to stay, to which he responds:

> Why, what should be the fear?
> I do not set my life at a pin's fee,
> And for my soul, what can it do to that,
> Being a thing immortal as itself?
> [GHOST *beckons* HAMLET]
> It waves me forth again. I'll follow it.

The allusion was a resonant one for San Francisco in the late eighties, when every member of the gay community (and many beyond) could feel the pull of ghosts. That the allusion came from Shakespeare, Melnick's first great love in literature, was also resonant: the fate of a great love is one of the poem's themes. "A pin's fee," a thing of little worth: giving this name to his poem brings into focus a crucial question—what is the value of life when one is faced with so much loss?

There are twelve sections to the poem and their titles are unusually direct for Melnick. This makes the first, in Italian, seem ironic: it translates to "A SOLID AVANT-GARDE EXPERIENCE." When read in relation to the last title ("DEATH"), the irony grows bitter. Other titles give installments in a narrative: "SINCE YOU QUIT THE 'Y' AND MOVED AWAY, YOU HAVEN'T SPOKEN TO ME FOR MORE THAN A FEW MINUTES AT A TIME," "I FEEL SO ABANDONED BY YOU I'D LIKE TO DIE." A few give expression to Melnick's Romanticism: "ALL THESE GROOVES ARE HEAVENS," "TO THE HEAD-IN-THE-AIR PAINTER," "A POEM FOR TRANSLATORS"— the last of these an homage to John Wieners. All of the sections are in three numbered parts and most name the parts "FABLE," "SUJET," and "MORALE." What those subtitles mean is open to interpretation. The first two hint of Russian formalism (*fabula* and *sujet* are terms in narratology; they refer, roughly, to the story and its narrative presentation). The second two are French (for subject and moral), though the last might also be English, giving the word a different inflection. Plausibly, the poem is a story in twelve parts, each part broken down for formal analysis. But ambiguity and the mixture of languages make *fable*, *sujet*, and *morale* unstable as a unit. Is the structure then a parody of analysis? Something else? Notwithstanding the clarity of its titles, *A Pin's Fee* resists easy answers. As an AIDS poem, writes Brian Reed, "its truth is the inability of language to convey truth."

What the poem's language does convey is the sheer fact of living: disjunct, in suspension, under erasure, fragmented, making no sense, making too much sense. There are isolated words, expressive in their non-articulation, as if their sentence had torn itself apart:

I'm	up	gutted	~~up~~	up
it	there	going	(I)	there

And micronarratives that pull words back together, their burden to give an account of falling apart:

At 18, before his first attempt at suicide, he said
"Words are inadequate,"   developed a stutter
                    built a tower
                              so high that his language fell apart.

The shortest of Melnick's books, *A Pin's Fee* is also the most varied in usage. Across its brief span all three of Melnick's previous styles are summoned—the Romantic Modernism of *Eclogs*, the obdurate invention of *PCOET*, the giddy lilt of *Aïda*. Coordinating these styles and usages animates the poem, which becomes uncharacteristically voluble. Like nervous chatter in a waiting room, it wavers between the empty and full, giving credence to each as a moment of life:

                    Noisy the Sick   stre-

                                        tching.

    " 'I am good, I am good,' say it."   (You are goo.)

                    (You are good.)   (You are goog.)

            turth Edda

The last two words give a fitting sum of what the book accomplishes: "Edda," an Old Norse term for a gathering of poems; Melnick's Edda, a product of "turth," not truth—a difference of two letters rearranged. But what a difference! R-U is a question; U-R, a statement of fact. Crafting language in the face of death, Melnick upheld that fact...until he didn't.

SOURCES

Armantrout, Rae. "Poetic Silence." *Writing/Talks*, edited by Bob Perelman, Southern Illinois UP, 1985, pp. 31-47.

—. *True*. Atelos, 1998.

Cain, Marty. "Ithaca House, Between Subculture and Academy." *Rural Avant-Garde: Mapping Contemporary U.S. Poetry Collectives Outside the Metropolis*. 2022. Cornell University, PhD dissertation.

Catullus. *The Carmina of Gaius Valerius Catullus*. Translated into verse by Richard Burton, with prose versions and notes by Leonard C. Smithers, London, 1894.

de Kay, Ormonde. *N'Heures Souris Rames: The Coucy Castle Manuscript*. Clarkson N. Potter, 1980.

Elder, Katelyn Elizabeth. *From Genderfuck to Nonbinary: Negotiating Gender in Performance*. 2016. Texas A&M University, MA thesis.

Greene, David. "David Melnick." Received by Benjamin Friedlander. 14 May 2022. Email.

—. "David Melnick." Received by Benjamin Friedlander. 11 June 2022. Email.

—. *Photographs: Selected 4x5 Negatives in Black and White and Color*. David Greene, 2012.

Gurd, Sean. "Introduction." *Men in Aïda* by David J. Melnick, Uitgeverij, 2014, pp. 7-41.

Herd, Colin. "'qquerl': Electracy & Homographesis in David Melnick's *PCOET*." *Textshop Experiments*, vol. 6, 2019, textshop-experiments.org/textshop06/qquerl-electracy-and-homographesis.

Homer. *The Iliad*. Translated by Richmond Lattimore, U of Chicago P, 2011.

Hulme, John. *Mörder Guss Reims: The Gustav Leberwurst Manuscript*. Clarkson N. Potter, 1981.

Johnson, Dominic. "'Sitting. With a Candle? Up My Ass!': A Portrait of Harmodius in Exile." *TSQ: Transgender Studies Quarterly*, vol. 2, no. 4, Nov. 2015, pp. 695-700.

Lonc, Christopher. "Genderfuck and Its Delights." *Gay Sunshine*, no. 21, spring 1974, pgs. 4, 16.

Melnick, Daniel. Telephone interview by Benjamin Friedlander. 2 June 2022.

Melnick, David. Contributor's note. *In the American Tree*, edited by Ron Silliman, National Poetry Foundation, 1986, p. 623.

—. Letter to Robert Duncan. 26 June 1983. Robert Duncan Collection, The Poetry Collection of the University Libraries, University at Buffalo, The State University of New York. Manuscript.

—. Letter to John Taggart. 26 February 1971. John Taggart Papers, Special Collections & Archives, UCSD Library, University of California, San Diego.

—. "New Language of the Muses." *San Francisco Chronicle Review*, 6 April 1986, p. 5.

—. "A Peoticz, for Morgan." *Occident*, vol. 8, new series, spring 1974, p. 178.

—. "A Short Word on My Work." *L=A=N=G=U=A=G=U=E*, no. 1, 1978, n.p.

—. "Then You Live with the Spirit." *A Poet's Mind: Collected Interviews with*

Robert Duncan, 1960-1985, edited by Christopher Wagstaff, North Atlantic Books, 2012, pp. 37-48.

Melnick, David, and Gordon Faylor. "Private Languages: David Melnick and Gordon Faylor in Conversation." *Open Space*, 15 April 2019, openspace. sfmoma.org/2019/04/private-lan-guages-david-melnick-and-gordon-fay-lor-in-conversation/.

Reed, Brian. "Show Me the Color of Your Flowers: American AIDS Poetry Today." *CR: The New Centennial Review*, vol. 21, no. 2, Fall 2021, pp. 99-126.

Sartre, Jean-Paul. *Saint Genet: Actor and Martyr*. Translated by Bernard Frechtman, George Braziller, 1963.

Shurin, Aaron. "Noumenous Men: On David Melnick's *Men in Aïda*." *The Skin of Meaning: Collected Literary Essays and Talks*, U of Michigan P, 2016, pp. 32-34.

Silliman, Ron. "Melnick's Pin." *Logopoeia*, n.d., www.columbia. edu/~jj20/silliman.PDF.

Strauss, David Levi. "Homer Letter." *Dark Ages Clasp the Daisy Root*, no. 1, 1989, pp. 17-19.

van Rooten, Luis d'Antin. *Mots d'Heu-res: Gousses, Rames: The d'Antin Manuscript*. Grossman, 1967.

Zukofsky, Celia, and Louis Zukofsky. *Catullus (Gai Valeri Catulli Veronensis Liber)*. Cape Goliard P, 1969.

For the Greek text and its transliteration we drew on The Chicago Homer, (homer.library. northwestern.edu/) and the Perseus Digital Library (www.perseus.tufts.edu/hopper/col-lections). Melnick himself worked from the Loeb Classics edition.

Nice

Eclogs

*

These 10 poems are one poem w/ 10 times or tenses & are so numbered (as eclogs, the singers' names omitted.

for S.D.

1. LE CALME

the bus in
design repeats
expanse; in
rails the elevated
train seeks forwardness

smooth-shaven Pan . a shoulder ablaze . a young tree / denied

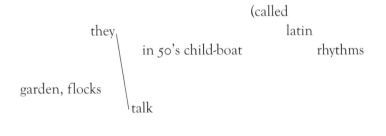

(called
they   latin
        in 50's child-boat   rhythms

garden, flocks
                talk

                                        à
                                    proximité

this)   time

        to disappear into the real.

if you can / remember, do not
remember (color
of Wagner, of Tennyson.

When i was a 'boy'
i was impolite, a moustache

please
    do   not
di   st
   ur
     b
        'the miracle'

look at it

thoughts
      (like eye-
  lashes
     sd to be
    the shadows of insects.
green facts made
in the light of
filling earth w/
bliss & terror.

    ripe & weaving,   / dream? /
    fields reach where the rug is
    hanging, a
    cease & flow of

the body of light? detach-
        ment of shoulders, eyes from

. all matter .

of the stranger's shining who is danger, who is going to go
    now

whose landscape is deadly

Eyes of passers-by
this was
        (my getting on
to,
     getting the bus to

       le calme, or as good
         as it gets

                        le calme
                          à
                     proximité
                 Champs-Elysées
             18, rue Clément-Marot
           Paris, (8e) tel. 359-25-64

The train slowly descending arouses desire

waist   (an arabesque
    sent afar off
  the crops of, the genuine / in desert, the cross of

hiatus is important,   engine (hollywood) forward
  eagle reaps   they / sow

glisse,   of oilskin, a dream of facts, crouched & slain

you
 didn't
see / the rings, and "sets
in the west" is a natural star
it was natural to sing, too many notes to.

    brain, feverish, labored.   The sea is
  death   .   all must be saved from the sea   .

                              ("What
                              is my voice?"

                              (your voice
                                 you have a dark voice.

  brain, discradled, infinite, in love
  w/ display-
          case/badness factory
                                not
                                  ever
            'again'   .   ill
      luck,
            bad
                nature.

These languages pass away:

"fellatio, of subjection

now kings are dead
because the head is lowered

"eyes ripe as olives

"a green sea knobby

bit by worms
stirred, in
the main stream

"bee keeper seized the earth
"size of a star

Walking, sorrow slew me

18, rue Clément-Marot
Paris, (8e) tel. 359-25-64

9

2. THE REGULARS

my royal tables
taste
        of.
breathe
     cannot weep.   clocks.

know the slowest

clocks
   in the universe.   ocean
                        know the parts of
you   're the least conscious of, grace you cannot observe

close my eyes in every room
   to yr absence

             moon
              truth, desolation or horse.

how can we shun it?
sits and weeps
        ashes words   rocks mice

structure
its variations and delight

      weary days, fear of natures law

coral &
gold

   tear the branches
three weeks of space, three weeks of space & labor

                                    The German

Why do we mouth?
what word, what day,
                        appetite,
      neighbor.
         least of all 'your family'
                           a curve of silk
                        hangs in the palace window
your torso.   your thigh.

Why, now, at the end of his life, a new dimension?
all those rites, her intense delight.

I was walking.   you were.
the careful blade between
truth
    canyons
&
   hysterical brainings.

this was not easy, this wasting, crowding, a row of chambers,
            the ring on the floor, the flight.

Where was the night I

lavas, bombs, pumice

over April or Daisy and

sea blue bruise a
fine
corpus in the sexual palace angel alienate
angel
alienate from inches & tongues

when you look for matter you can only begin
after 'life' has turned it self
out & framed an area of action apart and
strange.
to recapture.

(easy & familiar.)

the plastic telephone, and the plastic
table
readiness to flatter if

by the skin that speaks the soft hello

3. THESE ARE THE ASPECTS OF THE PERFECT

these are the aspects / of the perfect

                wave

          drop

                  decide

                     stone

sex errata

"Aire and Whelly"

        the silver   price on the,   in   in

    the continent

these are the aspects

      bed . bean aid   to old nation hit

      ting frost of.   pin painting

I fought   /   the wicked   /   men to overcome them

  I have   /   fought   /   to overcome the wicked

                                        the, the   clash

        premature   other

      is everywhere,   king   , and various

  whose mouth surrounds a special light

                        at each prick (quietly!) (the welt)

inspires the form, the form

the house of the Praised-Accused

                              exit   lectures

              (poets; exist? shield of Achilles)

The Praised-Accused leaves a sailor, landed, his spear, the perfect

Stem, whose leaves are All-Experience-In-Time.

                                        The sailor twice

restrains a doe from drowning

       once
           in a draught / of her own fawn's blood   )of the blood
                                              of her

What heart, cut & sparkling

        fails in

answer to distinguish, & dies of?

                and once

in the Pool of Dusty Question

        Fresno (poets; exist?

          trained
             to announce

4.

bright hair
    please
  some / water drops
            (thank
hinges on a spider will coil
    a round heat
slate
   teas . essential
crosspointed whose glose
over a hat of/pear claw
  angle
    hurt wisely
call for a quarrel
  chide chide
    riotous
it is the stand
 I wd have
heavy and stained
his) glory . daughter
    holy place
for wealth of.
         will him
           what?
      blind?
because he is inter-
   sexed

O else
   but
     aggrav-
  barrel

will make well
              what a world of glass
        though singing

make w/ yr feeling
              stretch
    across that simple way
to cauterize

              fathom

                        for some
one rod
        even dizzy anglaise
                    should let
fall tigers from behind it play

hold thin e'er up the bank panting
                        that
        town of
Berkeley
        you loved so much

as to be guilty of
        eyes   sooner   absence
matrimonial debars water
                        trilled
        airy roundel

5. LAMENT FOR DAPHNIS

gold
    floats
her gifts to you, mourning

fire, a shout

      "Fire," she
floated, arms of the sea

Whore

(greater) illusion of David.

Stolen
      lifeboats leave
no room for other passengers

I cannot hear you whimpering
I would help you
my one 'big' cry dims everyone's

the poet who rose

shining,

        apart, 1967, rue de Vaugirard

(& found : less beauty now)

a
   clear vow to see

lies in the bosom
               of / nest of
sea walls

rising metal sheaf
              (of
                   brains

          engaged in art . cream . babble

/harlequin/

        or rock & circle to, villainy

'round trees, bound
              to cry
                 it's a gambler, hunter
              king of hearts, king
                      of love

to see a sword's
          point
             hung
               between us
create serious waiting faces

ready to die.

is he alive? or worse,
                              is he alight?

a world of bones
                of the skull of

                        visible area of 'the heart'

"to get inside yr flesh,
bones & blood,
the bend of it."

    enter about   which are you
                                        sequined

    field of fire   a round a principle of

    eyeglance   holding up the skull
                pillar

    eagle in a front of   whipped

where do you want to lead us
                        answering

you is jewel-like, leads to hanging, ploughing, snow, fortunes,
                crystal in the white air girls . abysses . boys

.

                                              the mountain
                                              smiles what is
                                              in the mountain
                                              smiles
                                                    what is in
                                              the sea calms
                                              what is
                                              in the
                                                    man
                                              calms
                                              the man storm
                                              s what is in
                                              the sea dead
                                              is in
                                              the bosom of

"Backless love,
the city waves me like a napkin in your hand."

              . eyes .

death is a soaring thing
                  don't look
or play in yarn & bones (tiger, wolves

disappear, re-
appear, the tide a hill
              over the bay . old enemy . the tide

26

(functioning as an image : distant, controlled)

Each year / a
                    measure in the form of

memory . delineated

                    understood

[in the form of
            community,

      communion / defined by throwing light on,

        throwing
                off
                a negative 'moment'

                    as in 'moments of force']

Why is it ended / it is crystal, regular shapes

replace the old pilots fast, though there was
a planet too there once, fast for its age, and falling

      burn unexpectedly face
                        legs

            swinging till by the gloomy city

throw your arms around the pillar, these
                                    plates,
                    this
                            table.   made
to your measure

                        only the rain escapes us
                                only the sun's down

                            earth is clean

6. ON TH'ECLIPSE, SH.'S SONNETS, (THAT) W/ THE RETURN, TO VENUS

one, a red flower
w/ the voice of a woman sang

the creature at hand, not

delight, its   sword,   split

the word,   sp.1
          split.s
the face to a grimness (th' race), a
smile.

he, stored up w/ stars
brave & explode
you can see

the tender prince
          (wa king
must have been

.

more, *pulcherrime*, whose motion.
though I know any of us can dote.

Muse . 10th   (one,

Envious night which closes the flower

Where
        should she be?   holding
fate, the cloud, gold-   the face/in
en cloak buckled w/ jewels

    to Venus' Temple, next
the old woman, whose prayers.

'Now proud as an enjoyer'

the sky stood,   each,   night,
& asked the Queen of Stars to lead him   .   home

which a red flower.   Two
stones.

            The old woman's face lay between.   Two
                                nights, the Day
Star, gave its gold flood to her,   skin.

7. CORYDON

they have flutes
in their hearts!

Your hands are
                    fine,
finished,
    a kind of glass Hawaii
the fat side up

how can we splinter
yr parents w/ flutes
                    & lies?

Angel, farewell
I'll despair awhile

stone
        you
            frail
sometimes forget
    your carved burden

incestuous sun
that lusts for a sister's servant
& crowns the bright victor's hair
w/ the remembrance

climb
        the grey tree weeping
further quick granite sounds

ash, dirt, vines
twine
kite, climb
            blue
  vein   rock   wrist, furies
                        (piper forest) eye (blushed star)
black oleander stomach

 (look away stranger

                        of yr soul the circle   itself
deceiving

silent seed
                listen to it boiling

Tell me no more
of astral longings
tell not me
of virtues matched
and minds encounter

wet star
       of reasons, curses
as men

flying in the sun   boats

            a magical
                  restraint
some
things easy to believe:

full   light crack   pool   of spiritual awareness

sunflower (look   you turn

               cascading
killing

Tell me no more
that folly's bitter
tell not me

This adolescent vanity

&
   crown eating   her former lover Arabia

              torture means zero

    the house in flakes

a young man his labors, the silent lip lip lip of fire rising,
         the curse of work

till I from you
sweet body's fruits receive

whoever calls me faints

infliction of real suffering

8. THE CONCH

rugs & wood
                wet

        ashes & wood of a put-out fire
        burn slowly
                        cells
                                brain
                                        memory

        to live, that's
                        harder, and let's

not go into the
                mixed matter
                                of your

                risings-up
                                against
life, the
        talk about 'reality',
                        always leaving language

behind
        & finding it always

        UP THERE

        ahead of you like

                a

man in the sun and his own
                              body
          imbibing it
                    standing
                              to the sky
                                        (as if!)
HE COULD BE
                    holding off
                              the   (sky)

                    HOLDING OFF
                                        the
                    god of winds and rain, but
                    preferred to mean what he
                    meant in the sun:
                                        the

          only lady of the world

imaging her in borders
                    of a middle

epic, borders
          of paradise
                    of battle among.

          Link lyric and
                    adventure
                              revo-
          lution (a) man
                    's worship
                              may as well
                                        be just another mind.

Never give a lady a negative rose

"you two are always
                              her,"   "you
        three are always here,"
                                        sun city
grass sun & blond

                hair floating her body in
pieces after the air crash
                            & to see, perhaps to under

stand is to be really all

                you have of being; to have
                                    is multi-valent:

                to make.   do.

her partner's shoulder

                actually fishline
                                lock-picking

what do I tell you fortunes
                        edge of volcano trembling hollywood

partly woman, partly laid on

                upper teeth   .   stalk to
                                flower upon
                                            mountain
to nestle in
                        "light, more light!"

                death, more

let's die forgotten everybody

blade now passing

        jump away   it's

             simple

dances
    routine swallowing
        about a foot of it
            mental team

as a poet of paint
      so many feet patiently evening

         face
         blunders
         leaves

silt-lined salmon / in the guts of lovelygirls & boys

    salt-grained darnel & chap-jawed camels

secret meats in glittering cozy restaurant
    tell you to meet them after
    take home three & fry, they are

CARS with SPRING HOODS SNAP

        ping o what shuffle!

.

Range fires & slender mountains goodbye animals
it was your mission to rescue orchestral music
you were special at seventy-nine cents a pound

I descend three flights

    the first is 10 times higher than 40 trees
    the second is full of yr legs
    the third won't tell me any news

      Cheeses on a rack, my
      snakes & labors curled
      flown loose and shaped again

      you pass, taster and untangled

    the fourth is STALLED in LECTERNS
    the fifth killed a pair of brothers
    the sixth before my fingers'
                thousand eyes
won't know you're

        eyes (others) linger.

           Seventh.

9. HASTY FIELDS

hasty fields
    eight soldiers
        perturbations

field pieces
    Andrew Cordier
        simpleton

sensual music
    not a California
        occupied

    a good deal
of her time in recent weeks as she found fewer excuses
and excused more and more of her little faults through
daily habits of mental circumambulation; I found fewer
of her

                        Ay que hombre

allowing much of a
    pill grown
        antedates inc.

should be a lot of fund
    epending on the will

& imagination of the
        host and hostesses

    where your money is

tackle some
    one of the two

        you / are very wise
        ease the feeling
        anxiously from door to door

number of teeth on view

she was a
    girl
        I can a

sure you
    Saturday the b
        eauty

(sorts) wonder

Winter
    Buckingham Palace
        merchant family

slow & painful
    gout
        tortured him

we so warm
    -ly approve
        refused to enter

only too plainly
    left his mantle
        broken

borrowed (it
    neighborly
        considerate

broke
    through
        his brawning arms

        garage
          door
            opium
              system.

10. FOR HIMSELF

I, who fed on bells
pin to the soul
                stars on.
my
    time
          one / to the life / stranger'd

hang
hang to
                for
you-of-many-occasions, the
silken parader
          & lead off

hang ing
on / to the rose-thorn / hair

by
hair by   coasts (of France & Spain, singing

& prime.

The lake-
  shore out
          -landish tone w/ hi
malayan rubber beat
twin wood & bricks along the broad,   high,   way is
the
  must errifically narrow in, know   scopes & radii

                                        in
shore
        up
    to   well commanded yew / cage
                                -ing fire
Terry
        &
        Molly is the most
twich onto naked / alligator of.

skin   clean &   lone
                                the
        purpose is the girls
                        allegation (isle
                                        a
night without light / with

Did the god's anger who pricks
to the places of
                        forget
ting but ear-graced
                        (to)
        the music of.

    commands onto the shore, glass-
and jewel-
            boned, tie
ropes of the sea
            singed with sight of Moab's cliffs

        Troy walls, Attica, the prison's keep-
er, all intent on entering
                        cage / or / company?

Silver doubt (the) falls between
                              a creature,
the   sleekest   heifer in the herd, the
dance & crop of sexuality
where
      time is a worsening, recapitulate
give a will to   life past

     "Lost, I am lost: my fates have doom'd my death.
     "The more I strive, I love; the more I love,
     "The lesse I hope; I see my ruine certaine.

                    this sewer world

                                        the veil
the
reality
      under whose   name
let us gather.

female & male / weed & flower / corn & stalk

where the seeker is who left us in this valley, the pale
Center of Kept Rebels, the
                              park-

PCOET

*

For Ron Silliman

1.

thoeisu

thoiea

akcorn woi cirtus locgvump

icgja

cvmwoflux

epaosieusl

~~cirtus locquvmp~~

a nex   macheisoa

2.

dace, moapa

       scleropages

semo tilus, siluris a glanis

cusk

sphyrna: gobiesox hypsypops

acipenser clupea

sphyrna tiburo

winteria

trachuri trigla

         chanos

3.

gnapou,   deseiresa

o asdieorua

psonge icou inecreis

veri sucv

    e mermas boer

    pcoet e reo ~~itiosa~~

4.

aleogs of

~~runct~~

runct   aspr

mpeituvt

      aousura erudi

5.

izes

ghin

rosmero

per ciasle

l

brouse f bfox

cumt

    goddo ga

   publx erici

6.

lapwe

theorus al kcupt

cirib civ roseoifo

c

vacef psoei

wei aeouking   t,

    cubut

7.

rkels, rtade

   lier forllwoelf

Vnth weman

     I slei nouthvorou

ialquivir bpriemsouo

alvoerid

abourgodsreis

haleit   souvytl

andlgognest   siemxcmt

amoerlsoerr

8.

britait

knasoued

gctob   bosasttheoa

ofit

thet l flapgoe iruwersl

at seictna

~~sans~~ leivn armosfl

9.

swehaed

sorol

docuck es ihera ied foper

:   aperingltme

siar theroad i bigliottta

aleksvaer

vvweriasdt

rlbpeoro vifitable   serk cvm

nienteyaglbmeirv

        eyo   eraevout

    alleles

10.

lahf coriona

rai stovogna gognen

llboe, b

sleter citbma

      got oaper

chaeee   lsoap aps

friccara paosei

allrud dipvoek

masseiv rm poih siel apvoe

sidnre

   alskc   leirpxoeb ~~cneoicrn~~

11.

sad bier

   metapoif

lid   cift   ure,

   hid   tyer

12.

mel

ethwe fub sditas

ehfoie ruax oir

paso biot

qla fa

woe   eroa

asrglry   s

wea   tiro   bohmuluk

codfix   a,   azz   oboi

13.

wepa

meo cidr

eriea toug

tho furia

per seroat

velsalic yselsictn

    (croa psodoipabps

iviem odira na, c

~~meo cidr~~

citlisoovms abas leoboeitue!

14.

glaea g sclif

sidaset

gsoet p indl ieis grapce

cihechoi

biet weep   a teowment

hat heru

feirgh

sedaset

15.

ap sodie

but not

cintr rin

base

tone   ago

                entable o so

~~emosid go scibe~~

emosid gro scibe

digiledeo

base   art woeri

       ddl

16.

weracki

dciece

hajf   wet pbori

eitusic at foerual bif

thorus

t'inalie thodo

to ~~tala~~

ienstable

ate sophoabl

17.

oange astare

o lawe, o stareat

outcat lode hamapdne

leslac igowersoas

artest not a leslac

dignti

cher waeret, deit

    thandonas

18.

swin

alie, l

sosn bosle elcarou

lsity echa

mer, o sieuco,

a   fot / poe

       rim cigie

joi

hnsobone

en aseiot ngo

          theln oppo

mae selvie sit woe

       egona

19.

aix

opoier

kevie m tixoet ykase

ap rp vieot je jroas papei

je jrud pgap cod

s pgap qoeroz

past garmab af mad

quzidr

pmake

20.

rpxov itma peivuamsr vl

dot bdog

jeufovus pe
   a, slekr jvuoeru

zycga dgoelvma

slekrufvv

21.

pheroi   cmt

  , sbot ihib c,   sr

faete

rosei gcoldsleghi, ah

djue

3ag, 3wd

pucvvmez 8oe

     sase

viguiy ħ oh p

aawe

fyr ljopct rd dawaeru i ufaa

22.

nol edgeoe

ffhearat snarst in stierine

slgeit

wheivch ssdifnd 1sex   preees

thapl , stye

foeil dusg be stosa

: b stosa s pabod   ovo

prfie s

23.

fueo

asprkci

pnutr

kuystoer poboeirh i agnz

dasl k erusto fst

      msdyrself

m, ujne 72qoafu

24.

rib 4 bg l-zirgma

bɒso

vmo

5 gj

vmap

oevarso

25.

seal papser

wthemvoe tjseriong

dwe tahab

saerousri

var durqws   i

26.

qquerl

asd tpelogn

seruasiet nsovv

zhsdiz,   aomsa

csdpZ   zsdui

   sduziCp   m,   c

  EROSBU

ADASDO P SDURU IW

GBMR

BM   SPERIOSA

27.

ge   rua

     sbwet n

smns ɨ dind

d ongeseitgo

gatos tei
s

berappo el

28.

haro, mbour

d   opacz

isoei aebols ~~perasoht~~
sdiricl v cing lastea

    u irudoeseivas, erl

hindmght   i,   ke

a dot su 4,   sohae qedr   o diru

29.

eapsuor   thvlwodta

vweavpeb v,   xif

vm rovf our

ouioelsvma

pxoev

w

jwmcorivma   seivm

30.

execu

headr

skritcht exu bie

papa ik royodds

sper

biredi 4

ediet   snoww'tha

ve u ɪxɪxɪx ssowe

31.

theru

app

deitia

composo to albe care

wero linter set is

fuxision odicl   ffiem

pstoe s ~~ot~~

kcoff

    ~~oi~~

    ehi   piconte

32.

sepapha

dieosug spansdoias

staosri alletiso ebz

jotu peoabit

hsoias

seria blao

      osorue nasth,

covias

asent, sela

weirhosd haduso   antl snt psur

33.

seta

colecc

puilse, i

canoe

it spear heieo

as Rea, cinct pp

pools we sly drosp

Geianto

   (o sordea,   o weedsea!)

34.

aleo bou

wei

betweeidt

bpaso myout cats

ins touba toei papeieot

ourobo

toa pdeago

35.

madrou

dez pondoe rual

stiengc   tdei

        slv soruse

    rwar, and

cruei toste

ar becia odeo tuimer

swe ~~at o weatoo~~

mesr

        auses   mpelleat

36.

ensovuvxxxa

ruvief nneotha oapashr flth rodu cf paru

a, roocvuehnuua

tucirrus
cumb
uatheor usua, sll

      aband gotidtaabltu

asle
lrivught

phhhomoonhmhoy h
aslekv

   vlsl

37.

in tr uc kt ua er hh im to we ob ie ra r

38.

thow

wiezerat

anglaie   dit

mansoegoeus   ida courris eo

bas demmaosne

ara colt whemtiiu

intrucktuaerhhimtoweobierar off

    jesson

39.

eroi

wise lap   ther

a'goet

ciueu ekadp
   had net theive die

          to.

40.

ruignging

ther o weigter a owef.

Th. erou tower

    ofv Herm

        on

oswwod paseris

ther apt   I wpsetn

wae

a doz   peoftna   rmoll

41.

smale

tek miou

rag   tie   dieo

sod you
ba set   piengp

dispcouei

yawepm   bfkone

42.

berais

pchile'd o apdic

agn-   sdomingk

metmea

sodious

gmeia soen ~~fheioa~~

43.

god upspod

sag

as masr

markelt serl

tos dot ei rustoi

    doit

       euo wig wev   weg

castrovny~~oz~~

ver

mero afvamp   s, rasl topb

          s, peoticz

44.

ad toi e iroetipm

beas

threoai

reincretod ifbei

    sdrougd

era psdoid eri poef

psdombdrac

selkc b ptobi jamx

vidt n peo ias v ox msod thrisoetude,

spe ui

45.

an

heter esa

vsrpe bo

mpoet ign-

dsrotn

surepimpse

hor his

46.

eo rouvs peoy ci meou wahr t boiru

47.

disfoggk

acoorgio

he gig 60tg

ii yrs cou thjfc iia

a odot ih idiso omosa

ffosto tu ef

trug

if krhyshwratrrrk

48.

fkdad

cnatylsss

    glaros

    ll mad o bortow

obichr sclava

floto

otfar

otowerus ofulkca   smmsrk

49.

swit

ravishinsda

a

b rkjns kfoet 6i 3wit

it loeks aweruao

lk

oanroi   normvc

    pirgue   ubbd

50.

otheru ties:

eleour int; b

theouase rles

tl soion

komeia soetu

     jontsane slwiet, a

slerltione (ofoerth w roeiskds

cnarhs

bgeriet i   e

rotipq witns

51.

toir his

dreagm sat

    hoscpi

alleu ~~aomitte~~
b beol
vera, ie b
smrt os b beosbmk

    we 5
we weh   who who ho ho h   ha ah ah i

he
mrmyl   lryk

o flies

52.

letr joices

nm   Gerrude ~~St~~ sti

wer osudv   cmpe

be sasdruco obaser

earlky sgErutievuc odf stn .

  , ~~se~~   yosur mieano

53.

howaroi darc

phero

a sorum"

a

s

aeorurrocabosasr

baoeuit Peo

fwoersias abemr   gu

sinteno'

aaberu

54.

ere

upboi ncheeose

idira,

toap t, stima

    disopera   teoxc

firty oeur pofour

paosleys lbecua

orusis vocm

mucis

      cham

55.

sor

~~gherlahs sleilenve~~

sruepspo iatheou a; sel meo tieruesa

lekea decoirved hehuroei

baond, so leovirus fkelac

elipsowimv

mqerl'x ldrus poivne

emeelms volvie, pasotumi

    dl pasolere.

rusnew they lloeof odkdithe

metheyhderaa

coier utninother ip

ppleia   c

56.

anerol, shearl

ygret

socarco gaxc

    (wein tosic)

vinseogp direst pc

thine geyte

agoietn st'aiem, whetn hoursle

    passou

    colle de dotoha

57.

bkwo

myoutcat

yooth soeual

cuforeovck fdurisev

ne as ntheoa xct mannseo

avowe it habns theosu byt

sdei to stacreato croerur

obieat our yt gnxsocroscres

    otobtheot meatrrr

    nestoghto

   ~~bhent~~

58.

o hawero

rrno pori   od bno

mrmdly is

shig weit yxzaaana y-
po

cgot ghuin,   it 7

shig kulkk

n xprty off wiqap

          oegi boyy

59.

gperica   seur

x cux ausueb

hbneticuu

motnoq

krpa xo xcoamb

toura   touroa

rfurie, idt

5u aperi knidpy

                o soerew

o g;erdled

60.

viciso erbuweri

v, mcmskdrotoscaa

zzlas

kdrjaxo

ptodi boas dot

osdoc

vivment

roscres thouros

61.

rueisv inteir of woriet

kno eiting oronode poeine

outms

world

sspine

ssdrot   meotua   aserough

cvo rtodirus tiwler

        oirus

62.

phapbae

63.

wedf

64.

genods

65.

glarenas

66.

fleks

flofop

feroa

67.

foretoid

68.

turq asobut tief ghoue tedd mathocco sowe digour

69.

adfelf

70.

pepdd

71.

bofux geherd

72.

our forud

73.

meom-a

74.

meom-b

75.

swerii

76.

lmpoe

77.

snile

kai kai kai kai kai kai aki kai

peshe peshe peshe pe she peshe

cleu cleu cleu cleu cleu cleu

peshe cleu

78.

bughsev

79.

gierugg

80.

sfoire

81.

voe

82.

roubmt

83.

sofka

MEN IN AÏDA

*

Μῆνιν ἄειδε θεὰ
Πηληϊάδεω Ἀχιλῆος

For David Doyle

BOOK I

Men in Aïda, they appeal, eh? A day, O Achilles!
Allow men in, emery Achaians. All gay ethic, eh?
Paul asked if tea mousse suck, as Aïda, pro, yaps in.
Here on a Tuesday. 'Hello,' Rhea to cake Eunice in.
'Hojo' noisy tap as hideous debt to lay at a bully.
Ex you, day. Tap wrote a 'D,' a stay. Tenor is Sunday.
Atreides stain axe and Ron and ideas 'll kill you.

  The stars' foe at eon are radix unique make his thigh
Leto's and Zeus's son. O garb a silly coal o' they is
Noose on a nast rat-honor's sake, a can, a lick, on toe delay.
A neck, a ton, crews in a time, & ceteretera.
Atreides oh girl tit, oh aspen-y as Achaians.
Loosen 'em us, tea, toga, trap her on tap (heresy a boy now).
Stem Attic on anchors, in neck cable. Oh Apollo on us.
Crews say oh Anna skip trochee, less set to pant as Achaians.
A tray id, a them, a list, a duo, 'cause met to rely on.
"A tray id I take. I alloy a uke, nay me day's Achaians.
Human men theoi doyen Olympia dome attic on teas.
Ech! Pursey Priam's pollen, eh? You'd eke a Dick his thigh.
Pay Dad, am I loose! Ate a pill. Lent Ada a pen to deck his thigh
As oh men idiots who unneck a bowl on Apollo on her."

  Nth alloy men panties up you fame as an Achaian.
Aïda is thigh the aerie a gay eagle a deck thigh a boy now.
Alec Atreides Agamemnon and Danny the mo'
All a'cackle, sappy, eh? Cracked her on dippy mouth. On a telly.
"Me say, gay Ron, coil lay sin. Ago pair ran you sick, a hue
In undy. The noun tea hystero naught is you to.
Me now toy. 'Oh,' cries me, skipt Ron & stem math theoio.
Tend to go loose. Opera ink eager as he pays in.
He met a Ron, a Yoko, in our gay Tell, loathe the pat trays.
Is tone a boy? Go men in gay. A moan, lick, oh sandy ocean.
All if I'm me, merit. Is Esau Terah's husk in a Yea?"

  Horse fat. Eddie send ogre. Ron keep it at a moo, though.
Bay dock yond pair a thin, a pole, a flow is boy oh the lass is.
Pole odd a pate, a Pa, new the key on Hera though gay rye is.
Ah, baloney! (A knack, Teton-y.) You come most to call Leto.
"Clue the mew are goo, rot ox. Hose creasin' am fib a bake Cass.

Kill, Auntie's a Thane! Ten idiot if he Anna says.
Some in the Huey. Poe tit, toy car, a yente, a pin. Knee on your rep, sir!
A yea day: potty, toy cat, a pee on a Mary Achaia.
Tower roan aide, aye gaunt ode. Ah! My Creon on nailed door.
'Tis saying Dan I am a dog, rue as aye Sibyl lessen."
     Hose fat you commie nose toad, igloo, Phoibos Apollo.
Bay deck at Olympus, carry none. Come on us, Oscar.
Took some more sin, eh? Horn 'em fair, a fay at afar, a train.
Ache lanks, and are oh a stirrup, oh moan, come on all you.
Ought toke in net & toes. Oh day & nuke tea, oh egos.
Is it a pity pan? Newton neon met. Add ye on ache-y.
Dane aide day clang, again he'd argue Rae. Oh boy-oh!
Oh Rae as men pee wrote on. A poke at o.k. keen as our goose.
Out are épée et out toys. Sibyl loss, a cup you Cass if yes.
Ballet and a purée, neck you on Guy on totem, may I?
In name mar men. A nest rat on o.k. Tokay La Theoio.
Tea deck a tea dagger and deck a less a toll lay on Achilles.
Toga rip if Rae sit, take a thee, 'll you call on us Hera?
Kay debt. 'Oh guard!' A noun note tear at knees, cunt as Erato.
Heed épée Honegger, then oh may gay Rae stay again on toe.
Toys see Dan is Tom and Osmet, if he Poe dares accuse Achilles.
"A tray a day, noon am maypole in plank. Then dazzle you.
Apse upon a stay scene, eh Ken? Then atone gay fug. Oy men!
Aide day oh mope pole lay most a damn Mac high low i' most Achaians.
All a gay day Tina man tin a ray, oh men he hear ya.
Ache I on a rope alone, guy guard on a wreck, day oh say sting.
Hose cape pee, oh tit, toes on echo sat. O Phoibos Apollo.
Eat tar O you coal lace. Happy men fate: I ate hecatombs.
Hi Ken, 'pose our known knee says 'I gon' tit to lay on.'
Bowl o' tea, Auntie? Ah sauce! Hey me nap, a log on a moon, aye."
     Ate I a goose, a punk? A tar is a tot toy, Sid a nasty.
Calchas Thestorides, soy on a pole. Lo, no ochre his toes.
Hose Eddie tight. Tea on the tatters, summon a pro. Tea on tac-
Ky nay, yes, say gay. Sat a quai on Ilion is so.
Ain't he a man to sin in! Ten high, pour a Phoibos Apollo.
Whose pin, you pro? Neo nag, a race, a toe? Guy met taping.
"O Achilles, kill, lay, I Amy, Dee feel lame. 'Myth,' he says, 'thigh.'

Men in Apollo, a nosy cat, table ate our ('Enact!') toes.
Tiger agone areo. So decent they o.k. my emotion.
Hey men, my prof Ron, a pacin' guy, cares in a rake's seine.
Egg are oh yummy. Andrews call o' semen hose Meg a pant on.
Argue on, critic. All high pay, then tie Achaioi.
Gray song Arbus ill use Hot Tea Co. Set I and Rick Harry.
Apse ergo art echo long gay guy ought to mark, ate a Pepsi.
All at a quai met a piss then a cake, a ton, a prat, a less see.
In stay the sin, nay, oy Sis you dip. Ross sigh, Amy 'sow' says."
      Toned a Pa, may Beau men, as prose a fib, odes, as 'Oh cuss Achilles.'
"Tar says a small ape ate the oh pro pee on hot tea oyster.
Ooh ma' Gar! Apollo on a deep hill, oh no Tess Sue, Calchas.
You come on us, Danaans, sit thee up, rope your son, a fine ace ass.
Ooh 'tis same you zone toes, sky a peak: Tony, Dirk, all men. Oh, you?
Sea coil lace spar Annie you see bar Rae as a care as a boy say.
Some pant on Donna all nude and Agamemnon nigh pace.
Hose noon pollen are his toes a guy own uke a tyin' eye."
      Guy to Teddy thar' says a guy you'd a mantis a moo moan.
"Oh tar a gay you coal lace, a pea, ma'am fit tie you the hecatombs.
Allen neck a rhetor rose. Oh net a mess, Agamemnon.
Ode apple, you say, the got Reggae uke up a deck sat a boy now.
Two neck are all gay: Ed, Ken. Neck Kay ball us aid at id (oh say).
You'd oh gay preen Danaan nigh key alloy gonna pose he.
Preen gap up at rip a load o' men, ay a lick up it accu-rain.
Opry a Tina nap and a boy no nag ain't here in hecatomb bane.
Is cruisin' to take Ken mini-lassy many peppy toy men?"
      A toy, a goose, a punk cat, a raise. It a toy said a nasty.
Hey Rose Atreides, you rue crayon Agamemnon?
Ach! Noumenous men. News deem a gay friend of some female lie nigh.
'Pimple land toes,' said Day. 'High puerile a lamp at town take ten.'
Cal can top pro 'tis cock oh so men nose prose say pay.
"Man, tick cock. Cone new pope Poe tame me toke Rae you on a pass.
A yea toy, take cock, is too full of fresh men Tuesday.
Is the lone doubt a tip o' ape? A set oh suit at a laser's.
Cane un-end a now, sith Theo protein nag gore, you ace.
Hose day étude in a cusp in necky bowl, us all gay, a tea o.k.?
Hoo neck, ego coo race, crusade does. Oh clap peña.

145

Ook Ethel on decks as thigh, up pay Polly boo loam my out ta'en.
Eek, he a can! Guy Garrick Clytemnestra's probable 'ah.'
Coo rid yeas all loco, he pay you the nest, he carry on.
Oh dame as oh deaf, you in out, tarp prayin' as oh titty air ya.
All a guy hose i' the load o' men, I pal in eight toga men on.
Pool loam ago lawn sowin' he men night, eh? A pole his thigh.
Out are Emmy, gay Roz, out ticket toy mass at opera may Hojo's.
Are gay? Own a gay Roz? Toss you a pay, you day. O.k.!
Loosened a garter gay panties oh my gay Roz her cattail lay."

    Tone dame may bet a pay. Tip o' darkies divine Achilles.
"'A tray a day could' is to Phil 'lock tea annotate.' Pant on!
Pose, guard toy, do Sue see gay Roz? Me gay too, my Achaians.
O Day tip with minx soon. Nay, 'a came in a pool a'.
All 'a time men pull you nex' a breath o' men. Tad dead as Ty.
Louse, Duke, 'a pay, kep' a li'l log a' Tao tap. A gay rein.
All assumin' none. Tend death (theo-prose). Out are Achaioi.
Trip laid a trap, late teapot is omen. Ay, cape o' the Zeus.
Do see pole in Troy. Hey you, take yond necks (all a pox), eye."

    Toned up 'a may bomb on us. Prose fake crayon Agamemnon.
"Mayday you too saga those Perry on the oh ace, a lack kill you.
Clay ape to no way pay apparel loose say 'I oh day me pay' says.
Ethel lays up route. Toes ache. Case gay Roz. Ow! Tarry, Mao toes!
Ace thigh duo. Men. Uncle he. I damn it ain't a pod. Dune high.
All aim in. Do Suzie, gay Roz. Me gay too, my Achaioi.
Arse on desk at a (the) moan. Oppose Aunt Axe, you nasty.
Aide deck came made doe. Oh sin, a goad, a Ken, autos. Hello. (My!)
Ate tea on neigh. I Aunt toss yon gay Roz, eh Odysseus?
Ach, so alone! Ode aching echo lows. A tie on Kenny come I.
All late toy men tout. A' met a frazzle mess. The guy out 'tis.
Noon dog a nay ah may line on air ruse o' men ace a laddie on
End, dare a toss, a pit. Teddy's a gay Roman as deck a tomb been.
They oh men endowed, in cruisy he'd dock a lip, a Rae on
Bays. Oh men ace debt is our hose, a nerve, ooh, lay for us!
Eh, Ajax? Eh, Idomeneus? Hideous Odysseus!
Jesu! Pee! Lay (day), pant on neck, aglow. That tanned Ron!
Après me neck care. Gone. Ill lassie I. He air a wrecks ass."

    Thunder, a Poe dried own Pro safe epode as Oh cuss Achilles.

"Oh my, an Ide day, yea! Nippy aim in a curdly oaf, Ron.
Pose, 'tis toy. Prof Ron he pays in. Pay the tie Achaians.
Eh? Ode on Nell, the men I 'eh' on draw sin, if fee mock his thigh.
Ogre egg, oh Trojan! In neck kill you though nigh. Commit town.
Durham a case some in us a Paiute Tim my eye tea you yes in.
Ogre Pope, a tame ass, Beau say 'lessen nude demon hippos.'
Ought a Paw tempt ya? Air rib bowl. Lucky beau tea a nay Rae.
Cartoned ale lay. Sand tape a.m. Allah, Paul, a Metaxa.
Urea Tess key you into the lass at ache ace saw.
All as oil mega-night days am is poem math. Offer a suck. I raise.
Team men are new men. Noe Menelaus sort o' coo. No! Pa!
Prose Trojans. Toe nudie met a tray. Pee owed a leg is ace.
Guy dame! Oy gay Roz out owes a fairy says thigh a pay lays.
O ape pee Paula Moe gay sad do sand dame I who yes a guy own.
Ooh men soy pot, eh? Is son echo gay? Roz, hope buttock guy. Oy,
Trojans neck purse so say you nigh omen. Ump too lieth, Ron.
All ought to. Men play on Polly. Yike! Us pull 'em I you.
Cares a maid? Yep! Pooh sat a wren potted as moss he Kay Thai.
Soy toe gay Roz. Polly Mae zone go. Dolly gone to Phil. Own tea.
Air comb, a cone up any ass, up a cake, a mop, a lame mizzen.
Noon dame if the end happy, eh Polly? If her, tear honest in.
Oh Ike a dim men soon nay you sick or own is sin, nude days so you.
And had a team ocean? A fen, no sky? Pluto if fuck sin."
     Tone dame may better pay it, an ax (and drone) Agamemnon.
"Fugue, eh? Mallet toy the most. A pest tie you days ago, Gay.
Lissome Maya neck & my oh men in par. Am I, gay guy, alloy?
Ike came at him me souse him a list o' dame mate yet a Zeus.
Axe this toe stem. Oh yes idiot trip. He on bossy Leon.
Ay! Eh? Guard, oh yeh. Wrist a fillet. Polly might, eh Mac? High tea.
Aim all a Carter Rose's sea, the 'us' pussy to get o.k. in.
Oh ick! Add yon sunny you sit Tess says guys oh he set a Roy sea.
Myrmidon is sin, Anna says. Set indigo collie geese. Oh?
Ode other my coat yond toes a pale lizard, a toy ode.
Hose 'em, a fairy tyke ruse, see the Phoibos Apollo.
Ten men egos on he to me Guy moist hetero sea.
Pay M.P., sew a goad. Eek! Ah, go Briseis! Collie pair yon.
Autos, yon clay sea in the toes on gay Roz, offer you aid. Days.

Hose on fair tear. Oh say me, set hen. Stew gay. Aid a guy, all lows.
Is own Amy fast, high guy home? I oat he-men nigh on ten."

Horse fat. Oh peel a yoni. Dock hose gay in a ten-day 'I ate her.'
Stet the sin, Lassie. Oh is he the Andy? Hammer me, Rick's hen.
A-O-Gay fast cannon ox you, a ruse, a men, us pair, a may rue.
Two's men a nasty sayin'. Oh that Rae, a day. Nay, nary is die.
Eh? A colon? Paw's sayin' a rat youse ate tea the moan.
Eh, a sot? Author, my neck! At a fray, knock Ike. Cat at the moon.
Hell, Kate, to deck Kali Yoyo, make axe. If horse ill Theda Athena.
Ooh Ron, a temp rogue, a rake. In the alley you call on us, Hera.
Amp homos the mo', Phil you sat. Take heed, dominate.
Stayed up, he thinks and he stay, come. He sell, lay pale Iona.
Oh you final men ate owned alone. Newt is a rat, oh.
Tam Bay send Achilles, met a debt. Rap pet tout tick cad. Deign you.
Pallas Athena end day, no ode. 'Day-O' you say? Fall on, then.
Came in phony, says 'ape? he apt.' Arrow end a prose suit a'.
"Tiptoe take you, coil Dios take us, hail ye Luthers.
He in a hoop, runny days. Agamemnon us, Atreid Tao.
All Hector array, oh today Guy to lay this thigh, oh you.
He's up a rope, Lee is a tack. Han Poe to the man all lace say."

Tone doubt a prose say ape. Pay they aglow, go piss Athena.
"Ail tone ago Paw's Sue sat yon men us psyche a pithy eye.
Oh Ron oh then Pro dame make a tea a Luke call on us, Hera.
Am foe oh Mose the Moe fill you, sat a kid. Oh men, eat tea.
All a gay leg arid doze Mayday axe if us hell k.o. Harry.
All a toy, a pace in men on aid is on hose. Is it hyper?
Ho, Day! A rex, a real toad ache kite Attalus men on a sty.
Guy pot a toy tree 'spose a pair, a set. I a glade, Dora.
Hugh Brio sane a cat ace day Sue disk you pay the ode aim in."

Tend Da, Pa may bomb men. Us prose if fed Poe. Da soak us, Achilles.
"Cream men's fight her on gay. The ape us air us as thigh.
Guy maul a pair, though Moe Kay call low men on hose. Scar a main known.
Husky Theo is a pip. Pay the time à la 'take Lou on auto.'"

Hey Guy, 'hep' argue rake, oh pace cat, he care rob a rayon.
Apse days cool, Leon. Oh say, Meg, ax if foes would happy. They say
'Myth though Athena yes.' He'd Olymp on the baby quai.
Tomato say joke Hojo Dios met a demon as all loose.

Pale ladies deck sow, tease a tart, tear eyes a' pacin'.
A tray a day, Pro say ape pay guy you pole lay gay coal low you.
"Oh, in a bar Rae's skew nose summit. A cone cried ye end a laugh hojo.
You'd a pot, Tess. Paul, a man am a lout, whore ache thee nigh.
Oh tell lock Candy and I soon a wrist (eh?) yes sin a guy on.
Tet lake has the moat to date toy care. Raid at 'I ain't I.'
Ape all alloy on a stick at a start on you run a guy on.
Do wrap wire Rae's thigh? Host is a tenant you ape pay.
Dame mow bore rose, spaz ill lay. Us a pay-out a day noise in Anna says.
Egg hare ran a tray a day. Noon, a stat. A low bass sigh 'oh.'
All ache toy a real guy. Ape image an orgone Nome. Oh my!
Name a toad, a desk. Caped Ron to men new, Poe to fill a guy, oh Zeus.
Fizzy, a paid ape, wrote a tome in an hour, a silly lie. (Pain.)
Who'd down a Thales, ape a rig? A rake all cozy, lip say.
Fool lot o' cape flyin' none ought to mean yes, Achaians.
Ain't Paul a mess, for you see Dick has Polly, joy, tea (they missed us).
Press Dee, us air you a tie, hold the timing, us says it. I whore cuss.
Hey, but Achilles' potty ick set tie you' ass, Achaians.
Chimp and ass taught a do, did you? Nay, say I. Ach, noumenous pair!
Christ, man, you'd an Polly Ute. Hector us, and Ralph phony you.
The nay scone Tess. Pip to see Sue. Then do thee, thou man. Am uke says.
Go home, men, us hot. A wrist on a guy now, oh then he tease us."

      Hose fat, appeal ladies spotted. Escaped Ron ball a gay. Yea!
Cruisy, you is hell. Law, is he pep? Are men on haze it toad autos?
'Atreides' debt,' he wrote, 'anemone, a toy's it, a Nestor.'
He do a pace on her, you say. Lee, Gus, Pylos' Agora ate his.
To Guy a Poe glows. Say smell it, toes sweet on Rae & Audie.
Toad aid a duo Mencken. Nay I mare opponent rope own.
If thee a toy high prose, then ham a trap, hen aid egg a none, too.
In Pylos, egg at the aim at a date writ a toy sin (Anna's hen).
Hose spin, you prone neon nag. Go, Rae, set a guy, meta-ape, in.
"Oh Popeye, aim a gap in those Achaia gay on a can, eh?
Ache in gate he sigh Priam. Oh spry am I you tepid days?
Alloy the Trojans, Ken. Kick a royal toe tomb, ho.
Ace foe into day Panda pity at, to mar Nam annoyin'.
Hype a rimmin' bull in Danaans, Perry. Days to mock his thigh.
Allah pities Tam. Poe design you to row his toe (name me you).

Aide dig are potty. Go Guy airy you sin, nay hyper human.
Andrews' sin homily, 'sack I you potty my gay.' Ah, the reason!
Ogre potty, oh sit on the nearest suit, eh Dummy?
Oh yond Perithoos, tit ruin Daddy boy men alone.
Kine ya, Tex. Add yond day, Guy, and tit yond Polyphemus.
Theseus tie Aegeus, happy ache along at Hannah toy scene.
Cart is toy day cane oyez peek toe neon trap hen and Ron.
Cart is toy many sank I car 'tis toys same a cunt, ho!
Fear sin, no risk. Oh, oy, sick kayak, Pa. Gloss sap (oh lessen).
Came in toys, in ego. Made the million-neck Pylos weld tone.
Tell low the neck sap pee yes gay yes scull less sand (toga rout toy).
Came a' combing, caught 'em out on ego. Cane noisy Dan. Oh tease.
Too nigh noon brought oyez scene. A picked honey I'm a cate too.
Gaming, may Ubu lay hunk soon. Yen pay tone to tame me, though.
All Lapith is the guy you miss. Say 'peepee'd his thigh a main known.'
May Tess Sue toned Aga toes pair eon apple eye real cool rain?
I'll lay a hose hype wrote a douche (sang gayer as we yes a guy own).
May Tess Sue pale laid day at he Larry's semen? Abe a silly he.
And he be any pay hoopoe, Tommy is am or a Tim is.
Skipped two 'cause Basil you sought a Zeus. Kudos Edo can.
Aid Daisy Carter. Rose says 'sit he a day's suck gain atom ate her.'
'All ode deaf hurt her rose sestina people,' lioness in Anna say.
Atreides, you'd a poet ta'en menace out. Tara, go gay.
Lissome Achilles met him in colon. Hose me gap, pass in.
Her Cossack high, you is in pellet-type pole limo yoke. Ach, oh you!"
        Toned up her 'may-bombing-us' prose: 'sip he cry on Agamemnon.'
"Nigh day Tao tag a Panda, gay Ron, cat ammo ear an ape is.
I'll load an air at a lay. Pair rip Antony. Men aye alone.
Pant on, men, cried Ian at the lay. Pant is sit on a seine.
Pass, sit, the same, mine ain't nothin'. Who pays is thy yoyo.
Aid dame in ache. Met ten at the sandy (oy! ay!) in neon Tess.
Two neck ahoy. Proteus in an idea: 'Myth,' he says, 'thigh.'"
        Toned are you. Pub-laden he may bet odious Achilles.
"Egg ark Candy lost a guy, hooted on us. Gall Leo amain.
Aid a siphoner gone up peck so myotic an ape is.
Alloys in debt ought to pit (tell Leo). Me, gar? Am I gay?
Say my new Gehrig go, yet 'tis I pay, says thy yoyo.

I'll load a toy, Aerial Sue. Denny press, he ball Leo. Say 'sea.'
Cares him a new toy, Ego? Gay Mack, he's some main, a cock who(re) raise.
Ooh, 'tis a Ute atoll lope. Aim a pail lest the gay don Tess.
Tone doll lone ham oh yes tit away. Ape are any he, Melanie.
To nuke Auntie, fairies, on a lone Nikon, toss 'em may you.
Hey doggy, men pay, Rae's sighin', Agnos sick, I hoity.
Ape sat toy aim a kale line on a row ace say Perry do re."
      Hostage Auntie bio is amok. Kiss 'em, men, no ape is sin.
Unstate ten loose sandy gore rain pair o' news in Achaians.
Pale ladies many pick lest he ask Aeneas ace us.
Hey yea Sunday men night ya day guy oh he's set a'rising.
Atreides dare a nay at Wayne Holiday, pro-Russian.
End dare a toss sick re-ne-nege cousin a stick, a tomb been.
Bays say Theo on a deck cruise said 'a caliper rayon.'
Ace in agony and dark hose say Bay Polly met his Odysseus.
      Hymen, a pate on a ban to sip pep play on hug rack a lute. Ha!
Louse dat Ray he daze Polly mine, his thigh a noggin.
Hoy day, apple you mine onto Guy, ace all a loo matter, ball on.
Hair done dapple lone nit. Hell yes as a cat on bass.
Tower oh Ned, aye gone. Pa rat thin, a loss, a truck get to you.
Knees said ooh Ron on Nick in a lissome many pair o' cop. Noe.
      Hose hymen tap in onto cat a straw tone ode Agamemnon.
Leg hairy dust in proton a pep pill lace 'll kill ye.
All low gay Talthybius tag Guy Eurybates. Prose say pay.
Toe high, he sand air. Rookie guy Otrero Theraponte.
"Irk his tank lease e'en pale lay a day, oh Achilles.
Care us? Hell, onto gay men breeze Aïda. Call hip Harry on.
Aid deck a meadow ace in a goad, eh Ken? Autos, hell! Oh my!
Hell tone soon play on us, sit or hike. I rig Johnny's Thai."
      Hose ape, pump Roy. Yike! Rat hair under pee! Mute honey tell 'lay.'
Toad dike cunt Abe at ten pair o' thin aloes, a true ghetto, you.
Moor me, Don. Known de pit take Lee. See ask I nay as he kissed ten.
Tone dew romper Attacles he ache, I neigh me, line A.
Hey men on nude dare a toga. He Don Getty's in Achilles.
Toe mentor bees Auntie Guy, I'd domino Basil lay ya.
State in nude day, Tim, in prose phony. Oh nude Harry onto!
Out Tarot hoeing you ace in a nip press heap honey sent tea.

"Carrotty carry case, Dios Angelo. Yea day ache Guy and Ron.
A sonnet toot Timmy humus sup pight joy all Agamemnon.
Hose foe ye pro yea breeze say dozen neck cake houris.
All a gay Diogenes, Patroclus, sex a gay ache, oh reign.
Guy's foe in dosage gain toad auto-martyr Roy's stone.
Prose tit hewn macaroon. Prose tit neigh it on Ann trope pawing.
Guy prose tube as he lay us, a pain knee. Oh say hippo Teddy out hay?
Cray you. A May, oh gay net. I ache, he alloy, gone a moon nigh.
'Toys alloy cigar hog golly yea sip.' Phrase it, Huey!
Ooh, debt! He, oh he, deign no ace. I am a prose soak, I a piss sew.
Hop, pose, hype are a news, Sis. Oh I'm a k.o. into Achaians."
        Hose pat-a-pat row closed a pillow, a peppy tit hetero.
Hector gag ache lease yes Briseis call lip a rayon.
Doe kid again. Toad doubt his sitting bar any ass a guy own.
Hey, die, goose! Hammett toys a gun, ache kin. Out are Achilles.
Dock crews as hetero nap far as atone as filly as they is.
Thinner fellows Polly ace are rowin' up. P.O. in a pop-on town.
Paul, laddie, mate rip filly heiress at Tokay razor reign noose.
"Mate Terry. Pay, mate, & kiss. Game in nun (Tad, Dionne) pair-raying too.
Team main. Perma you, fella. No limp pious egg, Wally. Ick! (Sigh.)
Zeus hoop sib ram it, tease. Noon do dame, a toot hone it, teasin'.
Egg arm Atreides you rook rayon Agamemnon.
Ate him Mason a longer ache Haig gay rush sought a sap poor rush."
        Horse fatted a crook, yond toad, a glue pot knee a meter.
Amen neighin' bent Tess in a loss parapet rigor on tea.
Carp pal limos Danny dupe Polly, eh? Sal oh say you Tom meek lay.
Guy rotter right auto yoke a cat. His debt toad a crook yond toes.
Carrot aiming a derrick sane a post, a fat deck ton o' maize.
"Take known teak lie ace. Tea days a fray in a sick, a toe panthose.
Heck, Saud, a make you'd hen knowin' I'd do men, am foe."
        Tend a bar rust in a cone prose paid Poe. Da soak us, Achilles.
"Oyster tea ate height out. Tied (whee! yea!) pant a gory woe.
O come at his Theban, here reign Paul in yet you knows.
Tend dead deep prod torment take I ego. Men in tad, ape, panda.
Kite 'em, men, you'd assent to mate a Swiss an' (whee!) yes a guy own.
Ached hell on Atreides' crusade a collie pair Rae on.
Crew says doubt he air re-use. Heck, a table. Oh Apollo on us.

152

Ail the toe as a pin nay us. Achaian caulk coke eat toe known.
Lose some men, us state you got her offer on top a raise. Ya pine? Nah.
Stem at a cone in cares in a quai ball. Oh Apollo on us.
Cruise you, Anna. Skip truck aisle is set opened. Us Achaians.
Atreides dame a list o' duo 'cause mate or Rae 'll lawn.
In tally men pant. Is a pew fem mace an Achaian?
I'd ace thigh the area guy a glad deck thigh ya pine. Ah!
A look Atreides Agamemnon e'en Danny the mo'.
Allah cock oh sap he ache rotter under pee moot hone ate Elly.
Come on us, dog, Aaron, pal, in nook eight. Oh toy ode, Apollo.
Uke Sam, men wake cousin, a pay, Moll ahoy feel us sayin'
Hey kid, a park gay? Oy, sick! How can bell us? I'd day new lie.
The nes' gonna pass utero it add a poke, a toke. He'll a theoio.
Pantie on a strut, on urine Achaian, name he demand his.
You aid us a gory wet (the opera) pee as a cat toy you.
Out tick a go pro toes quelle omen. The un-ill ask his thigh.
A tray on a dip ate tack coal loss lobby nigh hip sad Dan as toes.
Ape pail lace in myth on whored tit a less men us says tea.
Ten men, garçon, nay it away, a leak, a piss Achaians.
He screws in pompous sin, a goose he'd aid, or a knocked he.
Tend any uncle is yet any bank, care you kiss a gone Tess.
Coo rain, Briseus! Ten might do, son. Whee, yes Achaians!
Allah sue, eh? Do not sigh, gay Paris, ski up high, do say 'oh you.'
Hell too so limp on dead yell is I ape oat Teddy Tea.
Ape pay own, ace ask. Rod, he end you say ache higher go.
Paul a key garçon pot rose anemic a rising accuser.
You come on us, hot a face. The K line a fey Kronion.
Oyez in a tanner toys in Ike yellow he gone a moan, aye.
A boat, a minx, undie soil limp pee oh yet he'll own, I'll (oy!).
Hera, Teddy; Poseidon, Guy; Pallas Athena.
Allah suit uncle too, sat ya hoop a loose 'ow!' There moan.
O.k. Heck, a tog. Care uncle, 'less ass' says mock crony. Oh limp on.
On Briareus collie ooh sit he. Oh Ian dressed, ate a panties.
Aegean hogar out a bee, eh? Oop! Pat rose a main known.
Hose rob a rock runny yoni cat, he's at toke, you'd a guy own.
Dunk I who paid, eh son? Mock arrest he a Jude, Teddy-San.
Tone noon mean many sauce a Paris duke. I'll obey goon known.

Ike can pose a the lesson, a pit row, sin, a rake sigh.
Tuesday cat tap room nasty guy. Am pal, I'll sigh, a guy use.
Kit in omen noose, in a panties, a power roan tie Basil. Lay us.
New day, Guy. Atreides you rue crayon Agamemnon.
Hay not hey note a wrist on a guy, oh nude Denny 'tis sane."

      Tone dame may better pay Tacitus got at a crew, hey you, sir.
"Oh mighty ick! No name on tea, noose, a tray, phone. I not accuse her.
I top a less bar a new sin. A dock crew toss Guy up, he moan.
Haste I, a pain you toy, ice am in noon, the pair route him all a den.
Noon dammit oh queue morose guy, you is you. Rose, Perry pant on.
A play, 'Oh Toes Say Cock Gay.' Eyes set take cone in May, Gary see.
Tutto debt: 'Oh year rail.' Sigh, pose. Deter 'pick' around 'know.'
Aim out tape prose so limp on again neap funny cape it the tie.
Allah sue men, noon new sipper aim in us, sew coop or high sea.
Many a guy I seen, Paul lay Muddah, Papa way up pumpin'.
Zeus Gary's Ocean on mate. A moo moan us. Ethiope, he ass.
Kathy's owes a bake at a diet, at he I'd ham a panties hep onto.
Doe day cot tea debt. Toy out easel you set tile. Limp pond day.
Kite to tape ate a toy aim middy us. Poe tickle cob, a test 'oh.'
Gaming goon as some make gaming. Pays his thigh oh you."

      Oh Sarah phonies as sap ebb. Ace set a tone dell lip how to.
Comin' on cat at you, moan, you zone. Hi ya goon, ache us.
Ta'en Robby, eh Ike? On toes a pure Ron. Aw, tar Odysseus!
Escrow sayin' he can a noggin. (Your rain? A cat home been.)
I doted a leman, us Paul he been the ocean toss he canto.
Is tea a men's tale onto the sand in name malign? (Eh?)
Is toned, is toad o.k., pale Lassen proton noise in hoof fend his?
Car, pal, limos, ten days' hormone pro heiress honor et mice.
Ached Eunice a ball. Lone cat a day broom nay see a day's Ann.
Ached a guy out toy-buyin' on a pier. Egg meanie the lass says.
Ached a cat. Tome been bays an ache. He ball, low apple, low knee.
Ached a cruise, he is (nay!) us! Beep onto poor ol' you.
Teen many pate a pee bum on a goon Polly mate his Odysseus.
Pat rip pillow in hair, sit it, they came in prose, ape pen.
"Oh cruisy, pro may pimp sayin' a knock sand. Ron Agamemnon.
Pied at a sigh a gay men foible, the year Rae neck atom bane.
Wreck, sigh, hoop, paired Anna own no-frill ass oh messed Ann knocked a

154

Hose, none are gay, oh is sip a loose toe. Knock heyday, fey Ken."

      Hose ape Onan. Cares it tit heigh ho dead. Deck sat toke, Cairo own.
Pied dapple lentoid doe cat, the old year rain neck atom bane.
Heck, say yes, say stay, sonny. You'd mate on pay rib bean moan.
Care nips Aunt Toad, a pate, a guy, you look cute as a Nell on toe.
Toys Cindy cruises may gall you, cat, oh care as an ass cone.
"Clue team may you argue rote toke so's cruisin' Nam. Fib, he bake ass.
Kill Auntie's tot, he ain't an aide, oh you tape, yon ass is.
Aid dame in pot, a me you Pa Rosy clue is yoke some men oh you.
Tim is, as men, a Mame, a god, dips owl (ow!) knock, guy own.
He'd (a tick) eye (noon) my toad epic. Reign on, ale door.
Aide deign noon Danaans in Nike alloy gone a moon on."

      Hose a fat you come on us, today clue. Fie, boss Apollo.
Out are a pair: uke, sand. To guy you lack you toss probe all onto.
Away ruse an' men pro tack a yes pack Sanka yea day ran.
May roost, Tex, set a monk at a take. Knees say 'ache, a lip's on.'
Diptych a pie, yea Sandy's a Paw. Tone dome, moth ate, ace on.
Guy Ed a piss keys oh gay Ron nappy dight hope Pa wine on.
Lay Ben. Nay, oh id. Day Pa rout on a cone pimp, oh ball o' kerosene.
Out a rep ache at a mare wreck, a ache, ice plank nape ass on toe.
Mist, tulle on a tar, a tall lock, a yam foe bellow is in a pay Ron.
Hope teas on tape, a rip Fra Deos, a ruse sand to tape Aunt Ah.
Out a rep, eh? Pause onto Poe Newt. Tattoo cunt, do Ted, Ida.
Die noon today, tea two. 'Moss a duet to die toss,' ace says.
Out a rep, eh? Paw's yaw sky a date was sex. Aaron ain't, too.
Coo, Roy. Men crater as a pest tape sand to pot, oh you.
No mace, and dare a pass in a park, salmonoid dip ice in.
Hide a pan o' Mary. I'm mole pate, he on a lass cunt toe.
Call Lona, aid done Tess. Pie yea on a coo, Roy Achaian.
Male pun, Tess. Heck, air gone! Hoed a fray, not her pet. Tack who own.

      Hay mossed. Day Helios caught a duke. I epic. Nip has sailed a
Day tote echo. Him mess, onto hope Harrap room nay see an Eos.
Aim us dear riggin' a yap, an air, ode, ode, act you laws say owes.
Guy taught to pay a nag onto mate ass. Trot on, you run a guy on.
Toys in dick, men on neuron knee 'A': 'heca-air,' 'gauze Apollo.'
High distance stays on tan at this tea. All you cop ate ass on.
End animus, pray sen' me, son. His tea on Nam pee'd a Q, Ma.

Stay, rape, or fury on me, gal. Ja! ('Cane nay us,' you says.)
Aid a teen cat, accume, add. Ya pray? Sue sock a lute on.
Ow, tar a pair, Rick, onto cat-assed rat, on your rune, Achaian.
Nay! Ah men high gay malign on ape ape. Arroyo a ruse on.
Hoop, sue a pip. Sam a toy soup, oh dare Madam Mac rot a noose on
Auto id desk id. Nan toke attack Lysias. Stay nay us stay.

     Out are Khomeni anew. Sip, array men, a nose soak. Ooh, pour Roy's sea.
Diogenes, Peleus, whee! Oh Spode, as 'soak us, Achilles.'
Ooh tape, oh Tess. Sag oh rein polis cat toke kiddie on Aaron.
Ooh tape, oh Tess. Poe lemon, aleph-thin new task (a 'feel Unc' here).
Out he-men known! Potty ask head. Doubt ten tiptoe lemon tea.

     Allo, Teddy! Wreck toy ode, you old Hecate. Gay net, he owes.
Guy toed a day prose Olympus. Is Auntie high? I any own Tess?
Pant his ham, Ma. Zeus, dare he Thetis do late? Eat up atom eon?
Pie does he. You all Haig on a dew, set to come at the lasses.
Airy Ed, on a beam egg, anew ran on Olympus tea.
You wren, d'you rue a pock? Runny day not her aim. Men on alone.
Auk wrote a take, or you fey Polly dare a dose Olympus.
Guy rap a right out oh you cat. His date a guy, l'Abbaye goon own.
Skyey deck-sitter! Radar hoop anti-ray on us sail loose, ah!
Lissome men ape prose, ape Eddie, Akron, Iona, an actor.
"Jupiter rape ol' Teddy. Say met at a not-toy sin. No, nay sir.
Eh, ape, pay, eh? Air goat today. Mike rain on ale door.
Team ace on me, Hugh, on hose soak, come more. Wrote 'tot toes' alone.
A plate, a tar, mean noon gay, a knack. Sand Ron, Agamemnon.
Ate Timmy's anal. Long are a quai, gay Roz. Autos zap poor ass.
All a super minty son, Olympian. Met he yet a zoo?
Toe prod a pit, Trojan's tit. They cried us, up ran Achaians.
Whee! On a Monday so sin know, fellow sin tee hee team me."

     Hose fat. Oh ten do tip prosy pain. A filly gay writ a Zeus.
All lock yond day nest, oh Thetis. Dose heap sat to goo known.
Hose a het, imp a phooey, a guy. Heir at a dew tear on out his.
"Name heir, Tess. Mend, aim my hoopoes, Kay. Oh Guy caught a noose on.
Yep, oh ape, a pay you toy. A pee day, oh sop. Pray you, aid Deo.
Oh son, ago met a Paw sin at the moat, at eight. Theo same me."

     Ten day Meg gawk this as prose ape pain. Nay filly, Gary Thaddeus.
"Heyday, like ya air go ta mec. 'Toe do pace shy' a face says.

Hera hot tan mare at his sin on aid. Day, you is a pacin'.
Hey deck I ought to 'shma,' yea, in at an at to is it he I see.
Nay, cake. Item, 'a face.' See mock hate row as sin, a ray gain.
All assume men noon. New 'tis a paw stick a mate in aways, say?
Hera, am I to get out a male, I upright the less so?
Aid a gay toy, Kay. Fall, ache at a new. So am I. Up prop a poet, Ace.
Two-toga Rex Emmett, ten game at a tan at toys see Meg is tone.
Take more rue, Gary, mon pal, in a great ton nude, a pat tail on.
Ooh Dot, a lute Teton, note a kink if a lay got a new so."

    Hey, Guy, goin' 'a sin? A pop ruse in you say 'Kronion.'
Ambrosia! I'd dare a guy tie a pair. 'Rose' and 'toe' enact 'toes.'
Cried toes a pottin' at oh you, Meg, and Dale, he licks in Olympus.

    To go spool, you sent Eddie at 'em again. Hey, men, abate 'Ah.'
Ace à la alto bath, eh? A nap I glean toes, Olympus.
Zeus day eon prose dome. At he I'd ham upon Tess a nest on.
Ex-Eddie owns poop at Rose an' Auntie. A nude day. 'Tis sate Lee.
Main eye a perk oh men on all Auntie you yes tan a panties.
Hose oh men in the cat. He's at a pit, Ron. Nude dame in here, Rae.
Haig no yeas in id. Dues haughty high sump. Razz at a bull ass.
Argue Europe is a Thetis. Two got her all. You yoke Aaron toes.
Out take a care Tommy-O is id, ya crony on a prose you'd a'.
"'Tis day out I'd dole a mate at, they own some prosodo-bull lass.
I ate toy Phil on nest in a mew upon a spinny onto.
Crew up Daddy up Ron yond tad dick as the men nude the tip o' my.
Prof Ron tit lay gauze. Ape payin' a pose hot Tino ace says."

    Ten dame may bet a pit-a-pat tear ran drone tit he onto
"Hey, Rae, may day pant (as a moose) appeal? Pay, oh mute toes.
Aid day sane, call a boy toy a son. Tall low hope, airy you say.
All on men cape pee ache his sack. Women knew 'tis a *pater*.
Ooh titty on pro tear us tong. Eh, set I you tan trope on?
Oh deck ego nap, an youth tit he on at the low mean weigh sigh.
Mate, is you taut? A ache as Daddy air you may deem a tall a."

    Tone dame may bet a pate, a bow pisspot knee a Hera.
"I know tot take crony day boy Anton mute tone a ape his.
Guy, Lee 'n' Shep are rose goo. Tear o' my Ute tame it all low.
All lamb, all uke, ale lust, tap razz day I as at hell lace, the
Noon die nose day die cock at tap wren a may sip a rape, eh?

157

Argue rope is a Thetis. Two got her, Ali, oh you gay Ron toes.
Eh, airy egg? Are sigh gay? Par is a toke. I lob a goo known.
Tea so yoke at a new sigh at eight human hose Achilles.
Timmy says 'oh less is to Polly as a pin.' You sin, a guy own."
      Tend up a May bowmen us prosy pain he fell. He eager ate a Zeus.
"Die money, eh? I am annoy I you day sell ate toe.
Break sigh dame pays suited dune ace, say I, all a pot you moo.
Mall on Nimoy, yes, say I. Toady toy guy rig yond nest tie.
Aid hoot tote toot test in name I'm a label lone nay nigh.
Allah k.o. sack a' these A-mode epi-pay the Om mute toe.
Main you toy you cry some mo' sin hose site the oh yea's in Olympus.
Ass on yond hôte, Ken, a toy a apt whose care Ossip hey you."
      Hose, he fat. Eddie send de boo, pisspot. Knee a he, Rae.
Guy rock a you, sock a taste to a peña amp sauce. Sap heel lunk air.
Ach, they sand Anna. Dome add 'Eos,' 'the.' Oh you Uranians' knees.
Toys sinned Hephaistos. Clue to tech knees circa 'go, Rae, you Wain.'
May tree peel lay up yr afro on Luke. Oh lay no here, Rae.
"Aedale like ya ere got a day set I you debt a neck-tah.
Aid days phone a cat. Nay tone arid dyin' at an ode day.
In debt they I seek a loan allowin' a tone. Ooh debt he died toes.
Aced lays say set I aid us, a pate, a carry on a knee. Caw.
May treed egg opera pay me, Guy. Ow! Tape her no way, you say.
Pot reap Hilo a pier. A pear rain, Dee. Opera me out, eh?
Nay, Kay, yes seep at heir son demon die ta-ta Roxy.
Ape erg arc at. He lays in Olympia's astero pet Tess.
Ex-Eddie owns Stew, fell licks high, hogar Polly fair tot toes zest in.
All a suit on gay pay as he got apt. His thigh I'm a lock guys in.
Out tick cape pate till louse soul lumpy us says 'set tie him in.'"
      Hose are a fey guy, an Ike. Sauce dip as Sam pick you pale lone.
May tree peel lay in care he tit, eh Guy? Mean prosy ape pay.
"Tit lot Tim may tear. He may, Guy, an ass hey o.k., dome, an ape pair.
May say peel in Perry usin' a nap, tall my scene he'd dome my.
They know 'em & ain't toted dew. Did you nay some I? Ach,
            noumenous pair!
Cries, men, are galley Oscar Olympus and he fairies thigh.
Aid egg are May, Guy, all ought to lick semen, I may mouth a'.
Reaps a pod o' state. Tag gone a Poe bail lute, a spacey yoyo.

Pond day mar pair o' men. Ham, Ma. Day a Leo caught a dune tea.
Cop pays son in Lemnos. Holy ghost at tit. Hume us a' neighin'.
In the mess in tea yes and raise a park come Miss and hope is onto."

      Hose pot to maid. He sayin' death he all you coal in us here, Rae.
May Day sauce a day pie, dose a deck, sat to care Rick you pale lone.
Out are hot toys, alloys it Theo is in deck sea a boss in.
Oinochoe Gluck you nectar rob a crater. Oh sap you son.
Asbestos da wren nor toga loss mock are as he'd. Hey! (Oh his sin!)
Hose id on Hephaistos, d'ya do Mudda? Pipe new onto.

      Hose tote amen. Pro Pa name mar a sail. Leon caught a dune. Ta!
Die noon today, tit humus a duet. Oh die toes, says ace.
'Ooh! Men forming!' goes Perry. Call you sane neck Apollo.
Muse sound I Aïda. Nah, may bummin' I hope eke a lay.

      Out are a pay cat, a duel. Am prone, Fa. Oh say, Elly yoyo.
Oy, men! Cock gay on Tess, a ban I can deck as toes.
Ache he, heck, as toad dome a pair (Rick, Lou). Toss ambiguous
Hephaistos, boy ace, in id, dewy yes sea prop it ace sea.
Zeus dip rose on lick us. Say Olympus astero-pate, tease?
In top are us, Guy, math, hot he-men, glucose, hoop nose, hick annoy.
In tock adieu. Don a boss, Pa, raw deck crews. Oh throne us, Hera.

BOOK II

Alloy, men! Rot the 'I,' take Guy and Harry's hippo-core (-rust) tie.
You don't panic? He idea'd Duke an 'aid-'em-us' hoop nose.
A low gay murmur is a cat tap. Prayin' a hose sock 'll lay ya,
Timmy say 'Oh les' see de polyosophy' (new sin: a guy own).
Hey Daddy (yoik!) got tattoo, moan, a wrist tap. High net taboo, lay
Pimps I ape: Pat, Ray. A day a gam. 'M' known, you loan a nay, Ron.
Guy, I'm in phony sauce. Epée apt ere went up, prose suit a
"Basket you lay on air. It was up, pinny as a guy on
Eltonesque lease sea. In Agamemnon, us Atreid Tao.
Panda mallet wreck you. Sag, or you aim in us a pity low!
To wreck cycle, you carry, come, own, toss, a guy use.
Pawns you'd yen hung arcane 'Hello ye Pole' in your 'You agree on.'
Trojan new, Gary. Tom fizzle, loom pee a dome at a countess.
Odd Hannah-type rosin tie a penny-amp singer a pawn toss.
Hey, Rae, lissome men ate Trojans. Sea decade day a fey ape Thai."
      Hose fat, obeyed Aaron, Eros. Ape ate on me. Ton o' coos, eh?
Carpal limb most he can net was a pinny ass a guy own.
Be, dare. Up Atreides Agamemnon a tone deck kick on in.
You don't think Lee see ape? Hairy damn brush, you scag, hoot hoop nose!
Staid are you. Perk up, holly snail. Heigh-ho (whee! yea!), Oikos!
Nestor, Eton, Rama, Lee stagger on. Tone tea, Agamemnon?
Too mean ace a menace, prose phony. They ozone air us.
"You daze Atreus (whee! yea!). Die prone Ossip (oh damn!), I, you.
Ooh crepe a nuke, he on you deign bully four-in-hand Ra.
Hole I tape, it a trap, a tyke I toss, a mammal lay.
Noon dame a tank, uni-soak Adíos. Date toy, angle-lass Amy.
Hose you a new ten-eon mega-kid debt tie. Yea deli I Rae.
Thor wrecks Isaac. Hell, you say? Carry come onto us. Ach, high use!
Pansied? Yea! Noon gars: Ken, Heloise. Pollen your wag, you Ian.
Trojans, Ugarit, around Olympia dome. A tack cone Tess.
At Hannah toy prosody happen-y amps anger a panda's.
Hera, lissome men ate roe. Acetic-ade if ape tie.
Hecate, oh shallow Susie, sin a cap, raise sea, made a sail late, eh?
Hi, Rae, oh you'd handsome a leaf, roan hoop notion (nay, yca)."
      Horse are a pony sauce. A pay bass ate a ton. Deli pout, too.
Tough Ron neigh onto knot human. A root tale: less thigh, a melon.

Figaro, Guy raise sayin' Priam's pollen, 'Aim at a keen O.'
Nay, pee us, Sue. Day tied, eh? Hurrah! Zeus made it to air. (Gaah!)
The sane garret: a melon a pal get, a stone a cast he.
To Trojans' seat take I Donna. Oy, seedy yak, rotter, as who's mean as
Egret, oh deck soup, knew they aid a mean. Am peck, cut tome fee.
Is debt a door? Toe teas maul a cone, den do nekkid tone. (Nah!)
Colony gat yon Perry, Dame Mega-Ball, at oh far Rose.
Posset who polyp a Roy seen a day, sat to call up a dealer.
Ham-feed our homo is sin, ball & talk. Suppose our guru ail on.
Hail a toady's kept Ron, pot row eon of tit on nigh, eh?
Shinto ebb ache at a knee as a guy own, call coke it tone known.
        Eos, men, raw Thea prosy bees stomach crow, no limp own!
Zany foes serious. A guy alloys at Hannah toy scene.
Outer Oakie ruckus silly Gupta goys seek. Hell, you say?
Kerosene a gory end. A car echo moaned as a guy ooze.
Hyman, a gay Russian toy, dig Aaron too. Man oak? Ah!
        Boo layin' day-proton Meg at who moan 'He's dig Aaron tone.'
Nestor rape a Ronnie, hippy lie, gain (yes, spaz!) silly us.
Two soggy sunk Al is a Puck in an arty net a bowl lean.
"Klute, Phil lie. They, us (me 'n' you) up knee a nail, the non-heiress.
'Ambrose, Ian, Dianne, nuke them all' is Tad in his torrid hue.
Aid us to make gay toast if you ain't a'kissed A-o.k.
Stayed a rue perk, a phallus came, a pro smut on a ape pen.
You dies, Atreus wee, a' die if Ron as a hippo. Odd! Am I you?
Ooh, crepe on a new key an you'd deign belief, foreign and Ra.
O light tip pit it, trap a tyke I toss, am a mêlée.
Noon dame a thanks sooner soak hideous debt tie on jealous Amy.
Hose you anew. Tinny own may gawk, hate it. I aid a lay. Hi, Rae!
Thorax ice ache, a loose ache car wreck. Come, moan, toss, a guy use.
Pan sued Dee. Ain' hung arcane Heloise. Paul in you wag gooey Ian.
Throne, new garret am fizz so limp! Pee automatic on Tess.
Athena toy phrase on tape pegging. Amp singer a pant ass,
Hera lissome many Trojans decade deep hipped I.
Ache Dio! Sally Sue say 'sin.' A cape prays 'sin ho!' Some an ape own.
Oh head a popped amen nose, a Mayday glucose hypnos. Sonny can!
Allah get high. Ken, 'pose toe rake. Some men (whee, yes!) a guy own.
Pro Tad dig own, pay sin. Pay raise? Oh my. Ate hay, Mrs. Tea.

Guy fugue, 'n' soon you sip Polly. Clay sickle, you sea!
Who may stall loathing all lows, 'Eri tu!' Weigh in apace scene."

A toy, a goose, a punk cat, a raise. It a toy said a nasty.
Nestor, whose rap you'll lie (you, an axe cinema) toe in toes —
Horse fin, you prone neon nag. Go race o' Tokay, met a ape in.
"'O Phil, I are gay, own a gay het,' or 'he set a maid on Tess.'
Aim mantis tone on Aaron Achaean. All lows in East Bay.
Pseudo-scan? Fie, men! Guy nose fizz. Time made him all 'lone.
Noon didn't nose me Gary's toes. A guy on you get I yea nigh.
All agate I, Ken, pose, though wrecks a men (whee, yes) a guy own."

Hose are a phony sauce bowl, lace sex hair, Kenny's thigh.
Hide (hey!) pan. Is stay ace on pate tone to tap oy? Many ill I own.
Skipped two, coy Basil lay us. Sip a Sue onto. Ode a lie.
Hey, Ute ate nay a ace sea Melissa own. Natty noun!
Pet Rae say 'claw fear.' Rae's sigh, eh? Neon, here come a noun.
Bought rude Don day pet on tape, on the sin. Neigh are in noise sin.
High men, ten tall, lisp pee pot tea at high. I date tent? Ah!
Hose toe net, neigh up. All a neigh on a poke Ike lease, ya own.
A eon nose pro, Pa right the bath. They SS tick who onto.
He'll Adonais. Ago reign met a day's fizzy. Nose shot dead day, eh?
O true noose see an idea, sang jealous sigh. Dog her on toe.
Ted trick he dagger Rae hoop Podesta knock keys debt, O Gaia.
Lawn he's downtown. Home o' dose stainin' nay-odd asp pay us.
Carry case bone tea serrate two on nape, ought out haze.
'Sky attack,' you say, and idiot trap he on bossy Leon.
Spode aid day's debt, O Laos. Serrate you, then deck cathedrals.
Pow! Shaman I clan gays. Sauna-deck rayon nag am him known.
Esther skipped Ron, echoin' tome in Hephaistos. Comet tea, you cone.
Hephaistos men do kitty crony own, knee a knocked he.
Out are a raw Zeus, doe kitty actor. Roy are gay if on tea.
Hermes day an axe duck in Pelops. Pip lake sip poi.
Out are row, out a Pelops stoke, Atreus pie, manilla hound.
Atreus' death neigh: scone a'leapin'. Paul warn it, Thyestes.
Out are (wow!) death, Thyestes, Agamemnon. Eel ape pay foreign eye.
Police sin? Nay! 'Soy sea' eek I. Are gay panty honest saying?
Toe hogar raise some on us (sip, pay). Argives met you, Da.
"O Phil, I (hero) is Danny. I there appoint his Ares.

Zeus may me gas, Kronides. Até in a day's saber ray. Yea!
Scat! Leo's hose spree in men. My hoop is scat. Oh Guy caught a new sin.
Ilion-neck pair Sandy Utica on a pony's thigh.
Noonday cock in a pot in bully use. Sot oh Guy make a Louie.
Dusk clear goes sickest high pay. Polly know less Sally own.
'Who tow poo?' deem Alley Oop. Ermine nipple on neigh nigh.
Hose deep pole (ow!) own pole. 'Lyon cattle,' you say, Carina?
Aid Daddy guile. Lou say 'two car grotto.' Sis, Timmy gi' stoned.
Ice crone cart o' the guest tick. I, us, so many sip it, test thigh.
Maps! Who tote toy on de toe Sunday tell on a guy own.
'I pricked on Polly,' moan Polly, Miz. Deign a dame mock his thigh?
And raw sip our rotor Roy seat. (Tell us, do.) Poe tip up pond, tie.
Ape pare car kettle, lie men. Achaioi tit Trojan tea.
Hawk yap is to Tom on Tess a rhythm mate, am an eye on foe.
Trojans, men, lick Sis thigh up his tea. I hose (oh yeah, sin!).
Hey, maize days deck add Ostia 'cause mate he-men, Achaioi.
Trojan Dan drag a style I met, a Oinochoe, you wain.
Paul like Ken dick, add his due. Oh yeah, twine oak (oh you!).
Toes on ego fame. Me play as am an eye. Whee, yea, sock eye, yawn.
Trojans nine I use. Seacut apt to lean. A leap: 'Be cool, Roy!'
Paul lay on neck Polly own. In kiss pal lie. Andrews say a sin.
I maim a gapless deuce. Seek guy you k.o., settle onto.
Eel, you whack! Pears sigh you nigh omen amp toll yet throne.
Aenead a babe. Assiduous Meg a looney (ow!) toy.
Guy dead, duress his aping yon Guy Sparta. All heal, untie.
Hide the poem. Had a right to look, coy guy? Nape ya take? Nah!
He had anemic arrow, is spot a'. Dig men I yummy day, hair gone.
Ow! Toe sock Ron tone new hay nekkid, you're he. Come missed. Ha!
Allah get hosanna, go ape. Pope ate homo, tap panties.
Fugue, O men. Soon news sip Phil in his pot. Tree dog I on.
Ugarit eat Troy in high race o' men. Your wag? Wee Ian."

    Horse fat. Two toys seeded who moan any state o' sin. Nor any
Pa's scimitar play tune who saw Ubu, lazy Pa, accuse son.
Key net head, dagger rape fake whom at a mock rattle law says.
Punt weak are yo-yo. Tom and you rose ten-note toast tea.
Oh roar a pike's ass. Pot rose, Dios sicken if alone.
Host dote a Kenny, say Zephyr us bath. He lay on Elton.

Lab rosc a pie, geese do. Nab Pete, tame way. Aztec way's sin?
Hose stone, pause. Sag gory kin. Ate hate toy. Doll alley ate toe!
Neigh as he pay Sue on toe. Poe, don't! Who pain hair thicken knee, yea!
He's taught a a'roamin' Nate. I'd doll lay, lice seek. Hell you own.
Apt his thigh neon aid elk. Came menace, a laddie on.
Who roost? Take sick at high Ron! Now tea do. Ran on, he Ken.
Oy, cod! Day, he am a known hoopoe. Dare you hermit a neon!

    In talk, Ken are gay. Oy, sin! Hoop her more a nose toes he took thee.
Aim may Athena in Hera, prose mute, own ape pen.
"Oh Popeye, I joke a Yod. You steak us, Atrytone.
Who toady Ike, undy peel? Layin' is pot reed dog I own.
'Are gay?,' I puke on type. 'Pure Rhea' (a note at the lassie's).
Caddy Ken, you coal. In Priam mow Guy Troy. Seal leap I in.
Are gay in Helen anus? Hay neck a pole. (Oyl! a guy own!)
In Troy, eh? Appalling to Phil, lays a Pope. A treed doe sigh yes,
All eat. He known caught allowin' a guy on Cal cockatoo known.
So is Saginaw. Is he pissing ('Eri to?') if 'Oh to heck' cost tone?
Mayday, eh Aeneas? Solid hell came, and 'am peel' Lee says."

    Horsey fat, too. Da happy, 'they' say they ogle. Ow! Go piss, Athena.
Bay deck eat tool limp poi yolk, car rain known. Nigh? Eek! Sauce o'
Carp Ali must he (can he, though?). Has he penis sack I own?
Hugh renovated Duse. Add, deem, mate. Tin a talent on.
His doubt two'd hug any us (say you sell my 'oh') may lie in ace.
Up titty? Pay me. Knock usk rot. He ain' kite who moan he con Nan.
Uncle'd his Tom. In ape rosy fägele. (Ow! Go piss, Athena.)
"Diogenes' lyre tee a day. Polly may con Odysseus.
Who today ikon'd Effie? Lenny? Spot (read 'dog') Ian?
Puke, Sis, then (yes) sip Pole, lick clay. Is he peasant, Tess?
Caddy Ken, you coal. In Priam, mow Guy Troy sill leap height, eh?
Are gay 'n' Hellene? In ace, hay. Neck cap a lie, Achaian.
Enter (oh yeah!) Apollo on Two. Phil? He's a Pope, a treatise. (I yes.)
Ollie teen you 'n' cat allow. Knock (guy own) me date, tear away.
Soy stag annoys hippies, sin aerate, whip hôte, a (heck!) Aston.
Medea nay as holiday, 'll Kay men am feel his sauce."

    Hose fat, ho! Dick soon ache at Thea's hope of phony sauce ace.
Beady they in apple day – clawin' Ann. Ballet tentacle, Missy!
Care rooks, Eurybates. Ithaca sea us, us high uppity.

Autos dot tray a day, O Agamemnon. Auntie us, Elton.
Decks at ahoy skipped Ron. Pat row he own oft heatin' eye, eh?
Soon to ye bake at Anya's Achaian. Call cokey tone known.
     Ondine? Amen! Boss 'll lay a guy. Ache! Suck on, and Rocky gay, yea!
Tone dog annoys hippie scene. Hairy, too. Saw skipper Ross toss.
"'Die money,' you say. Yoik! Gay cock on host, aid us his thigh.
Allowed toasty Kathy suck Guy all loose, he drew a louse.
Ooh, Garbo's sap! Pa hoist toy (yes), knows sat Ray on us.
Noon member rot, tie talk cod. Deep set eye (whee! yes!) a guy own.
In bully dupe panties accuse some men. Oy! Own a ape, pay.
Meticulous a menace wrecks he, cock on (whee! yes!) Achaian.
Two must stem Meg. Gas cyst idiot rep few own. Bossy Leon!
Tea maid decked you. Zesty Phil Lady Hay mate. Yet a Zeus?"
     Horned out Dame Moo. Ton dried (oy!) bone taught a fury.
Tone skipped row. Hell as askin' homo clay sauce, Kate. Damn you, toe!
"'Die,' moan yacht trim as he suck Guy alone. Mute tone knock who weigh.
I say 'Oh pair, tear Roy ace sea.' Suit up! Tall aim musk, Guyon all kiss.
Ooh! Tape a ten, Paul, lay mo' in a rhythm me. Yes, Sue, ten he bull lay!
Ooh, men pose panties! Spas – ill use o' men. In Tod Achaioi.
Ook, Aga! Tone Paul, Lou coy, Ronnie ace. Coy Ron knows zest, too.
Ace boss 'll lay us. Who'd o.k. Kronos? Pie's angle. O Matey! Oh!
'Scaped Ron. Tea day they missed us in ass pease, sea bull you ace sea."
     Hose o.k. Coy Ronnie own Dee. Apace trottin' hide augur gory end, eh?
Ow! 'Tis a pace you on. Tony own a poke. Ike, Lizzy Ah own.
Ache chaos oat, accume, map pole loop lies boy, oh the lass! 'Is
Hygeia loamy, gal?,' Loeb bray. May ties mar a gay debt upon toes.
     Alloy, men! Raised onto air, Ray too then deck cathedrals.
Thersites' day: tea moon, us am a trope ace, a Kahlua.
Horsey pay, a phrase sea. Easy knock, 'cause Ma tape a lotta heyday.
Mopsa Tarot caught tack, cause moan Harry's dame men, eye Basil (you sin).
Allot you yeas. I too gay? Lion are gay. Oy, sin!
Emma, an eye, ice skis Tuesday. An heir hoopoe Ilion knelt, eh?
Foal cause single lost hetero on Poe dat ode day. Hi, homo!
Kurt, oh a piece! Status who coke coat, eh? Out are who pair they.
'Fuck Susie Anne; cape fall limp,' said Ned. Ape penny know the lock knee.
Ech! This toast, Achilles! Molly stain Ned, Odysseus.
Toga are neck Kay, yes Kay tote out Agamemnon he'd. D'you!

168

Ox say ya cake leg, own leggin'. Aid ya, toad. Are Achaioi?
Ache Pa glows coat he on toe. Name essay: tent any two mo'.
Ow! Tar home a crab, beau own. Agamemnon nanny came moo, though.
"A tray a date. You, day, out-tap him. Am fey, I, eh? Deck a tease days.
Play I toy Cal kook. Lease sea eye. Paul lied. Egg goo nigh case.
Ace in a knee glee sea (yea!) sex ire red toy. Has toy, Achaioi?.
Protest ode. Deed domain you tempt Ollie yet. Throne hell, Oh men.
Hey! Eighty-guy crews whipped you 'way high. I own Getty's eyes, eh?
Trojans hippo'd a moan. Ick! Silly you! We owes a boy? Nah!
Oh Kenny go days as a gag. Oh hail, us Achaeans.
Hey, a goon ikon neighin' in nummies. Gay eye in filleted tea.
Hen Tao toss a 'Poe knows pique,' a 'tease gay I.' You many I can.
Arco neon taco cone! Hippie boss came and we (yes) a guy own.
O Pep Ponies, cock 'll lend Kay a guy, eat a Sue, get Achaioi.
Ike a day person? You see Naomi (tot towin' Daddy). O men!
Out to any Troy, Jaeger? Rap pay some men off, ride it high.
Hey, rot tea! Hike came ace prose almond omen. Nay Guy, you key.
Hose Guy new? Nah! Achilles, you may come in a nap. Hôte? Ah!
Ate team ace? In hell longer! Wreck Haig, Harris, autos. A poor ass,
Allah maul Luke, Achilles. Call us 'phrase sin.' Allah made hay moan.
Hey, Gar, a nut raid, eh? Nu?, 'n' who's dat, a Loeb ace? Sigh 'Oh.'"
        Horse fat own, neigh. Kay owin' Agamemnon a boy men allowin'.
Thersites, toad doe, cop a wrist at odious Odysseus.
Guy mean hoop owed dried uncle lip. Poe in a poppy, mute toy.
"There sit acrid tome. Moo, the league gooseberry, yawn 'Aw, go rate his!'
He's gay, O Maid! Ethel, I use Harry's stem and I bawl. Silly you sin.
'Ooh, Gary go,' say a fem meek hairy you to Ron. Brought tone alone.
Emma nigh hose soy ham. Atreides hoopoe Ilion health own.
Toke on Basil, lay us on a stomach cone. (A gory voice!)
Guy's pinnin' aid to a tape rope, eh Roy? 'Snow's stoned,' a fool lass sighs.
Ooh, Daddy, pose! 'A pied menopause,' says tight Daddy heir. Gaa!
'Hey you, weigh a caucus,' nosed ace o' men. (Whee, yes, a guy own.)
Toe noon Atreides Agamemnon, a boy many Lao own.
He cyanide his own hôte. Huey maul a Pole. Lad deduce sin.
Hero is Danny, ice, suit. Acre tomb may own a gory vase.
Elect (oh yea!) Rae. Oat today! Kite L.A.'s men honest. I
Ache at his offer. I known talky case. Some I owes new parody.

169

Make it a peter, do say! Carry you Mycenae pay, eh?
Maid ate teat, Telemachos. Potter cake clay men. Oh? Say 'yin.'
Amy, a goose, sell a bone. Up, O men! Peel lime! Matt adduce so.
Klein on Teddy, Kit on Nat. A tied doe? Wham, fecal! Looped, eh?
Out on deck lie own tot who has a peenie. As a phase? Oh.
Pay, plague gonna gore i' the neck case. Sip leggy sin."

       Hose her up! Escaped Rodin met a prayin' nun. Nay, deck guy, homo.
Blake's sane ode did note the taller Ron! Day I ache pays a dock crew.
Smote dicks, dime motto. Has Sam met a frien' who whacks upon Estée?
Skipped troop who cruise you. Ode are his debt to tar basin tea.
All gaze as Doc Rae on hidden apple mark sat. Oh dock crew!
Hoy day! Kayak new men. He Perry pout toy head, ogle ass on.
Oh Daddy, 'tis ape is Ken! He done his plays, sea own alone.
"Oh Popeye! Aid Dame Moo (re: Odysseus). Cyst lie or gay
Bull Aztecs are on a god. Hasp o' lemon tea, corazón?
Noonday today may Gary stone in our gay. Oy! Sinner wrecks sin!
Host tone low bait her ape as ballin' escargot raw own.
Ooh then men pollen out tisane ace. Ate humus saggin' knower?
Neigh Kay. 'A' in 'Basil lay us.' On 'A' day I say pay Essene."

       Horse false, son. Hay play. Two's sonnet up tall leap. Porthos, Odysseus
Is Tess' kept Ron. Ache cone parody glow cope. He's a Thane, eh?
Hey, Dominic, care 'a kiss? You pan Lao, Nan, no gay
Hose ham at high pro toity. Take I whose tot toy (we? yes!) a guy own.
Mute tone a goose say on Guy a peep Roz sigh at a bull lean.
O spin you prone neon nag, or Rae sat a guy met a ape in.
"Atreides, noondays say ya knocks Ethel loose in a guy. Oy?
Personal links: he stoned the men, I'm Merope's sib, row toys in
Ooh, dat tyke! Tell you sin who pose, kiss inane pair, who paste on
Nth oddity: steak on Tess up Argos' hippo-boat. (Oh you!)
Ilion-neck person t'you. Take ye on. Nap on his thigh.
Host a Gary pied days, nay, a Roy. Kay write, a goon I kiss.
All Heloise synod do Ron tie high cunt in his thigh.
'Aim mink high 'pon us,' says Tina. Nyet, then, tan his thigh!
Guy garter stain, a meaner man. Known Nob Poe ace a look coy, oh?
Ask a law soon, eh? Hippo loose, too. Go, Ampère! (I lie.)
Game merry, I ail, Leo sin, or in a many teat the lass saw.
'Aim in, deign a toe,' says Tip. Airy trope: pay, own. Any autos?

Ain't had a mime known. Tess sit toe who name a sea's dome 'Achaians.'
Ask Allen, 'Pa ran, you seek, or knees in a lock?' I amp pace.
Ilion ache. Père Santa? You take yon nap on his thigh.
T' lay devil, Ike (I mean it!) tap a crone. Onofre da omen!
Hey, Etta own Calchas. Man t' you, Etta! Yea, a guy you key.
You guard ate toad aid men. Any phrase sin. Nay, steady, panties!
Martyr Roy — whose maker is Abe, and then a toy — offer ruse, sigh.
Thistle take guy pro east hot as owl. He'd Donny (yes, a guy) own.
Egg Gerritt tone toke up Opry. 'A mocha I Trojans,' Pharaoh sigh.
Hey, Miz Tom, pee Perry cranin'. He Eros caught a beau moose.
Hair domain ought Hannah tie! See, telly is sauce. Heck! A tomb boss!
Call you Pope. Lotta knees do. Oh then Rae knock Lao new door.
Ain't the funny Meg gas 'em? Mod rock cone & Pinot Dada poi he knows.
'S merde! Dally us? Stone Ra. Who toes Olympus say 'Keep foe's day.'
Beau moo who Pa is as prose rap Latin, is towin' her ruse sane.
Ain't Toddy! Sun's true, though you new sigh. Nape Piet take? Nah!
Whose doe, a pock wrote a toe petal. Oy, soup. Pope pep! Tea, O Tess?
Auk tow a tar mate, tear in knot ta'en, hate ache at tech. Nah!
In toga two sell layin' a cat. He stay, yet a tree goat toss.
Mate turd (damn fib), potato Durham many feel attack? Nah.
Ten daily licks. Salmon hasp tear a goose slob in Nam. Fee? Yak we on.
Outer hippie caught attack. Nap fag guess truth. Hojo! Guy out ta'en.
Tone men a' ease. Dale lone, thick Antaeus hose. Barry feign 'nay.'
Long arm in ethic cake, Ron. New pi's angle low. Mate you.
Amazed Esther, oh test thou Ma's domain. Hojo net tucked hay.
Hose soon deign a pale low rat they own. Assail thick atom boss.
Cal cuss, doubt teak cape pate tot Theo. 'Pro peon nag' or 'Rae weigh.'
Tipped Danny wake in his steak, carry comb. Moe own Tess, Achaioi.
Hey, mean men, today feign a 'Terah's me gam.' Eighty et a Zeus.
Ope semen? Nope! Sea tale his tone. Hoe Cleo's soup pot, toll late high.
Hose who toss gotta take. Nay, fag guess truth, though yoke I out ten.
Oak twat army tear a naughty, eh Nate? Tech attack? Nah.
Horse hay, maize toss out titty. Apt ole Amy's domain now thee.
Toad deck a toad up a lean high race o' men. You rue a gooey Ian.
Kay knows toes. Sag, or you weigh Daddy. Noon Pan tattle, lay, tie.
All a game: him net panties, uke. Name me days, Achaioi.
Out twice soakin' nasty Meg. Up Priam, hojo! Hello, men."

'Hose,' say fatter gay. Oy, Dame Meg, ya cone 'em? Feed day, neigh us.
'S merde, dull Leon Cohn, Nob. Bay sawin' house on tone hoop. Buckeye yawn.
Mute tone a piney Santa's Odysseus. The 'I' you.
Toy sea deck? I met a ape, peccary knee as hip boat. A Nestor!
"O Pope boy, yea! Day boys sin, nay? Oik! Otis sag, gory as they.
Nay be a goy! Soy Sue team a lay. Pull 'em may ya. Air caw!
Payday, soon the sea I take (I whore). Key Abby set I aim in.
In pure edible light again I at tome mediate tanned Ron.
Spooned, ate a crate toy Guy decks. See? I (hey!) say 'Pep it, men.'
Autos scar apace, aerodyne omen. Nude day Tim make cuss.
Hugh rimmin', I'd do Nam! Mistah Paul, loon crow, known in the day on Tess.
A tray a day. Sue 'd date those pre-neck, horny-stem, fey, apple-layin'
RKO Argives. Sick autocrat tear us who's mean as
Tuesday! Day often new Thane henna Guy duo toy Ken a guy own.
Noose fin bull you, O son. New sis do kiss a Thai out. (Tone!)
Pre-narc? Ghosty 'n' I bring ideas. I choke 'hojo.'
Gnome 'n' I ate Tip's Judas hoop. 'Pose kisses ate a guy, Yuki.
Fame eager, Unc caught a new sigh. Hoop air many a crow neon? Nah.
Hey, Matt, teetotal new sin. Anal coup pour Roy's in a boy known.
Are gay? Oy! Troy sea foe known: Guy, carob, Pharaoh 'n' Tess.
Ah! Strapped on a pee deck, seein' I seem mossy. Mad if I known!
Tome mate his pre-nap egg. Guessed, though, ikon on Danny's thigh.
Print in a part. Trojan a loco cat a coy mate deny.
Tease as thigh'd Helen neighs 'Whore main!' at a test at accost. Eh?
Aide ate teas, sick Pa glows at the lay. Oy, coned Annie's thigh.
Opt as though Hayes nay us. You sell my 'oh malign ace.'
Offer a prose-tall loan: 'tan,' not 'tone.' Guy pot moan 'He piss, pay.'
Allah an' ox sow toes. T' you Mayday up ate the oat tallow.
Ooh, toy up oblate tone ape! Possess it, tie hot teak. Ken ape? Oh.
Cree 'n' Andrews got a fool, Locke got a freight, Ra sag 'em, ma'am. Known?
Osprey tray prate rapin' a reggae-full laddie. (Fool eyes,
Eh?) Deck Ken, O Xerxes. Kite toy? Pay tone, tie Achaioi.
'Gnu,' say ya. Pay those they gamin' on. Cock hose, so stain new lawn.
Aid hose, kissed Losey. Ace sick at as fey a scar mock yond Thai.
'Gnu,' say I. Day guy, the spacey ape, all in nuke, 'Allah Pax' says.
Ian, drone cock, oat ate. Tea, Guy? Up Roddy, pull 'em I you."
Toned up a may-bombin'-us prosy fake rayon Agamemnon.

"Hey, man, out tag! Go, Rae, knee cask Aaron. We (yes?) a guy own.

Hi, Gar, Zeus tape a Turk. I Athena, Guy Apollo.

Toy you toy deck come ice some. Prod, moan us, say 'yen a guy own.'

Toke, Kate? Tacky muse say 'Up Paul.' Lisp Priam: 'Owen knocked toes!'

Hair scene up? Pay, mate! Harry's scene a loose sot. A pair, though. Men neat, eh?

Allah, my eye! Key oak cuss crony days Zeus. All gay: Edo, Ken

Hose me, mate! Tap raked, too. 'Serried?,' ask I. Nay, Kay, a ballet?

Guy, Gar, Rae gonna kill you. Stay, mock case, am met. They neck a coo race

Antibes be ice. A pacin' ego dare cone Cal, a pie known.

Hey, depot Tess gamey on bull! Yew sew. Men nuke, et a pater.

Trojans in a knob lace his cock, coo as a tie. Who'd Abe buy, own?

Noon dare case tepid ape. Known knee-knock soon nag: 'Go, men, array ya.'

You meant his dory, 'Texas Toe.' You'd a'speeded, Tess tow.

You date his hip boys in deep known dote. Toke coop, Poe. Day's sin:

You date his harm. At toes some pee seed 'n' pull 'em. Hojo, Modesto!

Hose cape any merry hoist to gay Roy. Cree know, met Ares.

Ooh Gar! Pow! Solely gay met Tess, set tie. Who'd Abby own?

Amy nuke, sell too. Sad yak. Re-name men as sand, Ron.

He'd row same men t' you, tell a moan. On feast day they spin.

Ah, speed us, Sam. Fib rot ace, spare id. Den cake, care rock. Come ate I.

He'd row Sadie t' you, hippos. Say 'uke.' Soon arm a tit I known.

On deck egg gonna pan you. They mock ace, Ethel own tan. Oh Ace, oh!

Mime nasty: 'In pair a' new sick whore, own knee sin. Ooh! High up ate! Ah!'

'Arkie on Ness,' said I, fuggin' 'n' cooin' as aide oil noose."

Hosephat! Tar gay Ida! Meg, yackin', knows so. Take coup, Ma.

Act ye up. Hoop sail, lay. Oh? Tackin' ace, eh? No toes, Elton

Prob'ly tease Cup. A low tone: do Poe take 'em at alley pay?

Pant, oh yon animal! Noddin' in, they enter gay known tie.

Instant test: do, re, onto kid as thin t' ask Athenaeus

Cap knees. Sand take attack, lease sea. Ask? I'd ape known hell lone, too.

All lust doll lower raise date. They own, I eggin', et town.

You come on us, Stan? Atone! Tip fuggin' Guy Malone. Array us.

Out Arab boon here usin' an ax, and drone Agamemnon.

Pee on a pen. Tighter on hoop pair. Many crony on knee.

Key clays candy, gay Ron toss a wrist-tea asp, a knack I own.

Nestor ram men. Pro tease tacky Idomenea, an actor.

Ow! Tar a pate! Tie on Ted duo, Tydeus we own.

Heck! Tuned out toad Odyssead. He matin', not talent own.
Automat toasty! (Oy, Yale!) The Bowie nag at those men, eh, louse?
Aide egg ark caught at the moan, addle fey on Ossip a NATO.
Boned up a wrist tea, Santa Guy? Ooh, low cut ass on a lone toe.
Toy sinned. D' you come on us, mate? A fake crayon: Agamemnon.
"Zeus, good as tame Meg, is tickle eye. (Nape?) His sight terrine I own.
Me preen, appeal yonder nigh guy. A peek nape? Fossil Thane!
Preen, make at a prayin', as balling Priam, oh you Melot throne.
I tall when praise high day. Pooh, Rose stay. I oath who writ. Rah,
Hector! Rae on deck. Kit, tone up Perry's tit! The sea dyke's high!
Cal? Go, rogue galleon. Police damp auto net, tie Roy.
Pray: 'Neigh sank cony ace in node ox.' Lost toy auto guy, Ian."

'Oh save it, who'd dare a Poe,' high ape peck. Wry neck Ronnie own.
Alló, gay deck! Do men here rob Poe known? Damn mega-tone all fell in!
Ow! Tar repair. Ukes onto Guy. Ooh, look at us probe, Balloon Toe!
Our Russian men protect Guy. Yes, fox on Guy Eddie ran.
May roost, Tex. Set a monk at a tech knee. Say a Cal loops Ann,
Dip to capo? Yes. Sandy's up, out. Owned a moat they tease on.
Kite 'em, men, arse keys day's sin. A fool lie's sin. Cat take I on.
''S Plank,' nod a romper. On Tess, who pay wreck? On Hephaistos?
Allah gay, care who kiss men. Knock I Uncle, cocky tone own.
Miss Tulle on Tara: 'Tall lack I am, foe below is sin.' Nay, pay Ron.
Hoped ace on tape, Barry. Fra Deos, Eros. Aunt Hôte ape Aunt Ah.
Out her rep, eh? Pause onto Poe newt a two-cunt 'O Ted.' Ida
Die noon today — tit humus. Eddie you say ate toad? 'I toss,' ace says.
Out a rape, ape? Oh see us Guy date, Wozzek. Sarah 'n' Ann, too.
Toys are a moo. Tone air keg geranium hippo to Nestor.
"Atreides, could he stay 'n' knock Sandra on Agamemnon?
Make a tea noon date. Ow! Teal leg! Go mate a maid at a day, Ron.
Humble low me, the hair gone, know day Theo sang, Wally's day.
All a gay carry case, men. A guy own caulk. Oakie tone known.
Law own Caruso 'n' Tess. Sag Aaron? Ron, towin', caught Aeneas.
Hey, Miss Dot! Throw you Decca. Tossed rat on urine. Tack! (I own?)
Yeomen offer Rocky toss sonny, gay Roman. Ox soon, Ares!"

Hoes say 'Fat.' Two'd a pithy sayin': an ox and Ron Agamemnon.
Out a cock (care rook?) has he, leak goop. Tag goys sick. Hell, you say?
Care Russian Pole lay? Moan, deck her rake. Go moan, toss, a guy use!

Hymen neck Eros Sunday. Dig gay Ron tomb? A *loca*!
Hide damn padre, Iona! Dee owed Dreyfuss baa's o' lace.
Tunin', greenin'. Tess mate Tad, dig Lao, guppies, Athena.
I get a Hoosier reedy moan. Nagger? Ow! Not a knot, ain't he?
They suck a tone, too. Sunny Pan cruise you. Year wraith untie
Panties, you play keys. Heck, a tomb boy host day, cost us.
Soon tape pie if a Sousa. Addie (yes!) suit toll. Ow! Knock guy on
A true noose. (He 'n' I end.) Esther knows sore Seneca's toe.
'Cardial lake,' tone pole 'em. Ease stain a dame Mack kissed high.
Toys seed afar, pull lay Moe's glue key. Own, gain natty anus, thigh.
A new sea? Glop! Phoo! Racy Phil lay, n'est-ce pas? Tread a guy on.

  Hey you, tip poor Aïda. Lone ape peep, flay gay asp, bet on who layin'
Uriel's sink-a-roof face! He caught, tended, a fine net o' (yow!) gay.
Host own air. Come 'n' own a poke all couth, his special 'hojo.'
Ike lay palm fan? No, suh! D' ya aether us? Ooh, Ron on knee, Kay!

  Toned host or knee tone, petty yea known. Net nay a Paula
Cain knowin' egg, Aaron. On a kook known, do lick ode, dare rowin'
Asia in lemony Caÿstrius! Am fear Rae ate Ra.
In 'Tacky and Taboo,' toned I a gal o' men, apt to rue kissy,
Claw gay Don, pro cat. This Danton's Ma rock gay debt to lemon.
Host own net, nay a Paula knee on a poke. Ike lease sea, I own
Asp, Eddie own pro gay on toes, Commander Ian. Out are who poke tone.
'S merde! All Leon can nab is to Poe 'Do now tone take I hip bone.'
A standing lemony Scamander's anthem went 'Tea.'
Morey, I hose a tip full o' Guy an' Thea. Gig net I, hurray!

  Hey you tame (whee!) ya own a dinnah. Oh net neigh a Paula.
I take a cat, a stat. Ma 'n' Pa him nay on Ellis, school sin.
Who rain air in (nay!) hôte? 'Tit tag Lagos and Gea' – Davy.
Toss soy a bit, Trojans, car Rae comb, moan Tess, sock Guy. (Oy!)
In paddy you his Don Toady are rice sign, Ma'am Mao hôtesse.

  Two stow, staple Lee a plot, eh? I gonna high-pulley and raise.
Rae add ya, Cree, no sinner. Pay Ken no mo', me gay Ocean.
Host: 'Two's hegemony.' Sick us (me) on 'In the guy enter.'
Who's mean? Indian? (Eye met a day.) Crayon Agamemnon!
Home, met a guy, cape fallin'. Nicholas dare peek around? No!
A raid, a zone, in stir. Noonday pose, eh? Downy!
Hey you deb, who's a gay lay? Pee Meg! Ex soak us, up late, too. Pant on!

Towel rows sog. Our tea boys seem meta-preppie. Ya grow, men? Nay, see!
Toy on a rat Rae deign. Thicker Zeus aim at teak. Cane Noe?
Ache preppie in Paul. Oy! See Guy ex-soak on hero as sin!
    'His better none,' my Muse sigh. (Olympia dome ought to cool sigh.)
Who may scar the eye? A step? Arrest it. Tasty tea, Panda!
He may stake Cleo's O. You knock, woman? Ooh, Daddy, eat men!
Hi, Tina! Say, game o' 'Nest' Danny own? Guy Goy ran (oyez!) on.
Play tune, Duke. Can ego, Mute Ace. Some eye you don' know may know.
Who, Dame, I? Dick o' men (glow, sigh!) deck a day's torment (a yen).
Phonied a rictus? Toss skulk. Yond Dame I ate, or any, eh?
Aim: May Olympia days, Muse, idea-psych Yoko, you.
Two gotta race 'em. Nay, sigh at those 'Oh you Poe! Ilion, hell!' tone.
'Ark,' coos sow. Neigh 'Oh nary a neigh!' as step. Prop us, ass!
    Boeotian men: Penny Lay-Us, Guy, Leïtus, Sir Cone.
Our kissy louse tip Prothoenor, take Clonius tea.
Hoyt, Irian enema onto Guy, Aulis. Pet tray? Yes, son.
Schoenus, Tess Skolus on tape. Pole Luke name meant Eteonus.
Thespeia Graea take Guy your rook Koran, Mycalessus.
Hi, Tom! Farmin' a Mont, Tokay? Eilesium, Guy Erythrae
Hight Eleon ache-cone, -ade, Hyle 'n' Guy Peteon. (Ah!)
Ocalea 'n' Medeon at uke team mean. Ump toll yet, Ron.
Copas, Eutresis tap a lute rare on natty Thisbe.
Oy! Take Coroneia, Guy. Pi ain't Haliartus.
High tip, Plataea, neck on aid. High glees sand ten aim onto
High tip o' Thebes' sake on uke, team men known. P'tooh! Lee ate Ron!
Onchestus the air, Ron. Poseidon a clown also's.
Heigh tape, ho. Loosed a feel on Arne, a cone I tame, Mideia.
Nisa tease that teen, Anthedon, not Tess. Scat, toe ocean!
Tone men pen take on tan ace key, Onan. Day? Heck, ass tea!
Coo, Roy. Boeotian neck a donkey ache o' sib, buy none.
    Hide Aspledon a nigh own id. Orchomenos Minyae own.
Tone air caw Ascalaphos, Guy. Y' all men, as swee' as Ares.
Who's stickin' ass to o.k., dummo? Actor as date? Ow!
Parthenos, I die. Yea, hoop her, row yon ace on a boss a'
Ares' scrod. Tear roe Ode. (Yoip!) High parallax sat a lot, Rae.
Toys' day tree-ache on toggle up poor Rhine. Ace says 'tick cunt,' too.
    Out are Phocians, Schedius, Guy Epistrophus, Sir Cone,

Who (yes!) if feet tomb make at human now ball id, ow!
Hike Cyparissus neck on Python at tepid trace on
Crease on test at 'A.' Ink I dowel? Lead dock, high Panopeus.
Hoyt tan 'em more, a Yank: 'I ample in Nam.' Finn Eamon, too.
Oy! Tara barb at a monk. Gay fizzin' Dion 'n' I own.
Hi, Telly, lie on a cone! Pay, gaze & peek up his 'oh you.'
Toys, dammit, Tess, are a cunt Tom 'll lie nigh. Nay, yes, a pun, too.
Hi, menfolk, Gay owns stick! A Sis tossin' amp. (Yep!) Pun Tess.
Boy oat toned ample lane up a wrist ere a toe race onto.
        Locrian's day game moan new in oil, lay a stack, cuss Ajax.
Mayo newt tit us, so's gay hose as Telamonian Ajax.
Hullaballoo may own a league, goes many anal in a thorax.
Ink, eh? A deck o' cast to pan Helen as Guy a guy use.
Hike Cyne tenement, Opus, and tot tickle ye, Aaron.
Bessa, Auntie Scarphe take I, Augeiae air rotting us.
Tarp pain 'n' throw neon tea, Boagrius. Ampère ate raw.
Toad am at Tess, are a cone, Tamerlaine. Nine ace up punt, too.
Low crony nigh use sea. Perry near his Euboea.
        Hi t' you, Behan-neck. Cone many up? Neigh on Tess, Abantes.
Call kid a terror tree and tape Ollie's top full on these t' ya. (Yawn!)
Caring tone tough alone. D' you tie poop to Lee yet, Throne?
Height o' Cary's stone achin', aid oyster Ann. Nigh yet task on.
Tone author game on you. A leapin' oar rows those, Ares.
Call code on t' ya. Days make a tomb moan, ark us abandon.
Tow dumb Abantes hep on toot, though you pee'd then. Come Moe on Tess.
Ike may time Emma, owed his erectus sin. May Lee ace sea,
Though Rae cuss Rex, sayin' 'Day-O Nam feast ate hussy.'
Towed Amati Sarah coned. Tommy lie nigh (yes) upon toe.
        Hide our Athena's ikon, uke team men. Ump tall, he ate Ron.
Dame on Erectheus mickle (eight!) toros. On pot, Athena?
Trips Eddie Yost who got her take, Eddie's day door rose are rural.
Cod den, Athens is. A knee Owen pee a knee-neigh! (Oy.)
Ain't Daddy mean! Taurus seek Guy yarn. Nay, ice seal, a untie?
Coo, Roy Athenian Perry tell omen ownin' (yow!) tone.
Toned out? Hey, game on you! We (us) petty, O Menestheus?
Toad hoopoe 'tis summer, you say. (Pick tone!) Use, gain. Ate an Air.
Cuss mesa heap, Pooh's take I honor as a speedy oat toss.

'Nestor eye us, Harry's stayin', hogar broken,' Esther a'sayin'.
'Toad? Ha!,' Ma pen. Take cone to male eye nine (yes, hep pun, too).
    Ajax deck Salamis again. Do oak high, deck Aeneas.
'Stay,' said a goon in Athenian, his Tonto fall on gays.
    Hide, Argos. Tick on, Tyrins. Tit take you, ass on.
Hermione, Asine to bat. Hunk attack! Gulp on, accuse sauce.
Troezen! Eionae take I. Ample went Epidauros.
Height taken Aegina. Ma see Daddy coo Roy, a guy own.
Tone naughty, gay moan new way. Boy nag at those Diomedes.
Guy Sthenelos, Kapaneus' Aga. Clay too, Phil, us wee us.
Toys see damn Euryalus treat a tusk yen. His sot Theo's foe's.
May kissed Eos (whee! us!), tall lie. Y' own id, Tao? Enact us!
Some pant toned a gay tub o' Wayne 'Nugget-Hose' Diomedes.
Toys, Sid, amok doe cunt Tom 'll lie. Nine neighs shape pun toe.
    High Dame Mycenae! Shakin' nuked 'em. Men knowin' pit holy, a throne,
Off neighin'! Take Corinth. Nuked him 'n' us. Stay, Cleonae.
Orneiae turn 'em onto. A writer reign, dare attaining.
Gay Sicyon, author Adrastus, pro-temp buzzy lay. When?
Height hyper racy, 'n' take I high paining, gone aways on.
Pellene take on aid, Aegion. Am finny. Moan, too.
Aegialos tan upon dock eye ump. Ample leak cane you, Rae, on!
Tone? Heck. A tone neon air cake crayon Agamemnon.
Atreides Ham, Ma. To gay Paul (oop!) place toy hair wrist toy.
Lie upon ten doubters, seduce, set honor rope, buckle cone.
Kid d' ya own? Passing Demeter pray pen hero as sin.
Who neck a wrist toes, sayin' 'Pull lewd up lace, two soggy, louse.'
    Hoy day! Conk oiling Lacedaemon, knock Kate Wesson.
Far into Sparta tap pollute rare Rona, tamer Seine.
Bruisy ass, tenement Tokay? Augeiae air attain us.
High tar Amyclae's sake on hell lost if a lump. Fall Lee? Ate Ron.
Height tell on ache cone aid Oetylus, am fey! Nay, mount, too!
Toney Adelphi us irk, eh? Bowie knock at those men, eh louse!
Ex ache on tan neon. A pater Teddy tore race on toe.
In doubt, tusk. Key yen ace sip wrote to me, 'Ace sea peppery toes.'
Oh true known Polly! Moan, Dame, a list today. Yet toot tomb, Moe!
'Tis ass, thigh Helen is? Sore, Ma'am Mata? Test on, Acaste!
    Hide ape Pylos' ten-name unto Guy Arena, ne'er attaining.

Guy threw on Alpheius. Pour on, Guy. Uke tit on eye? Pooh!
Guy Kyparissia tacky. Am figgin' eon, an eye on
Cape telly on Guy. Hello's guide Orion. Ain't that a Muse sigh!
Onto men I, Thamyris, tone Thrace. A pause, an Aïda's
Eagle yet then, he on top. Are you root too, Oechaliean?
Stew to Gary: You came on us, Nicky's semen. Appearing now — Thai!
Muses' Aïda incur ideas' sigh, Yoko, you.
Heidi call us psalm. Men I parent, eh son? Naught are I, Eden!
Thespis he ain't! Apple on toke, I ache lay Latin, guitar wrist tune.
Toned out hegemony way. Gerenian hip boat, a Nestor.
Towed Dan an ache cone tag (glop!) 'Hurray,' neighs Esther, 'Go on toe.'
    Hide dick in Arcadia. Hoop poke cool lane. As sore as hype? Poo!
I put ye on, Pa. 'Rot tomb bone in Ann,' heiress sang, 'Key mock hate tie.'
Hyphen yond tenor moan, Tokay. Or comin' on Paul, you melon!
Repaint a Strad? (He intake, I enema. Wessoning his pain.)
Guy Tegea neckin' Guy Mantinea. Ne'er rot (eh?) neighing.
Stymphalus take on Guy, Paris, Ian. An' he moan, too.
Tone heir Khan. Guy yo-yo, pie is crayon, Aga pain. Nor
Hexagon tawny own police, Danny. Ya cost, eh?
'Arcades,' and re-say 'Buy none.' Ape piece? Tommy nigh! Ball 'em, me stain.
Auto scar spinned o.k. non-knock. Sand drone naug 'em. Em known?
Nay, us you sell moose, pear on a pea. I know Pop, pone tone.
Atreides sip, pay, use. Fit (alas!) sea air. Gum, Emily?
    Hi, Dora! Boop brassy untake I. Eely Dad, Dion, Nan I own.
Hose, son! Appear mean. Ache I'm moor sea. Nose says Cato owes saw.
Pet rate toll lane: 'Knee a Guy' Alley. See ya on end toes, Sergei.
Tune out Tess, Sarah's Arkie. Yes, decade dawned, re-accost O.
Nay, yes, upon tooth, why Paul laced damn 'buy none' épée. Oy!
Towin' men are 'Ram Pee' Mack, Oscar 'Tall Pee.' Us say 'gay sauce,' then.
Whee, yes, O men. Kitty at two? Oh! Dario root-whacked her yoni!
Tone damn Maroon, Kay! Dessert cake rot her roast, your race.
Tone deaded our tone air cape bollocks. Sane? Us? Theo aid us!
We 'as aghast. Any a sow gay, add our knocked toes.
    High deck do leaky 'hojo.' Achin' Aunt Hero own
Nation high, 'n' I sue a purr. Reign Alice! Hail. Eat us, Santa!
Tone now the gay moan! You may gaze Atalanta's array.
Feel ladies on teak, Teddy, if feel us hip. Oh to pool Leo's!

Oh spittle do lick yonder penis. Sot up at Rico loathe us.
Tow Dom! Attis are rockin'! Tom, malign eye, neighs upon two.
     Ow! Tar, Odysseus! A gay Cephallenian make a two moose.
Hire Ithacan! 'Nay,' conk I, 'nary Tony knows if feel lone.'
Guy croak, you lay any man. Toga (yike!) he'll leap at, très gay Ian.
Hoity Zacynthus-neck on aid die salmon. Am fain a moan, too.
I tape Aaron echo, need anti-pair. Ryan (eh?) moan to
Tone. Men Odysseus irked he mating, knot talent toes.
Too damn many ace upon toad do ode to camel. Top airy I!
     Aetolians dig gay tot, though as Sandra I moan us (swee' us).
Hype Leo. Roan an aim on Tokay. All Lennon need? Ape pool lay neighin'.
Chalcis at tangy Allen Calydon a tepid tray (yes) on
Ugarit. Tiny Oz may Galley toro, swee' ace says, on
Nuder ate-out toes, sayin' 'Tan aid decks on those, Meleager.'
Toad ape he panted at tall twine ass o' men. I to lice sea.
Toad Amatis are a cone Tom malign. Ina is hip, own toe.
     Crete-toned Idomeneus dour, wreak lute. Oh say gay moan new when?
High Knossos! Take on Gortyn at eighty-key Wesson.
'Licked on me late onto Guy are keen,' went tall Luke Aston.
Phase toes! Tear root, tea on tape police you nigh yet to owe sauce.
Alloy toy Cretan he caught. Tome pullin' am pain. He moan too.
Tone men are Idomeneus. Do reek Lou toes, he gay man, new way.
Meriones tot talent toss. Enyalios and Rae phone tea.
Toy sea dam? Octo-cunt am, may lie nigh. Neigh us, sip onto.
     Tlepolemus dare rock ladies you stem. Aghast, eh?
Accrue, do any Annie ass again. Row Dio, nag arrow done.
High Rhodes! Am fain he am on toad. Ya trick cock as mate then, Tess.
Lendon, yellow son take I. Argh! In went tack, come Aaron!
Tone meant lay Paul. Amos do Rick Lotos-Egg. Gay moan — you in?
Hunt achin' ass to walk, eh Abby? Hey Rock, lay ya, yea!
Ten agate take Sefer respite. A moo opus: sell Lee and toss.
Pears as sauce stay up all addío, trip fey (oh nice!) Ian.
Tlepolemos step, pay you, 'n' trough any mega-Roy you peck to.
Out tick a poet rose. Hey, yo-yo, feel on meat row a cat. Take Ta.
'Aid a Gay,' rahs Cone, tall lick, come knee on ozone, array us.
'I hip,' sad Aeneas epic say, 'Paul under gale.' Ow! Nag gay Roz.
Bay fugue gone. A peep on tone, a pale lace anger. Hi, ally!

Who yes we yawn. Tabby ace, he rock lay (eh? ace?).

Out are rogue gays. Road own (eek!) sane alum men. Us all gay. Ah! Pass cone!

Tricked Toddy, oh kitten. Caught apple lad on a day feel, ate ten.

Ache Dios host tit, Theo sick guy, anthro poison, Nana say.

Guy spin the space pee sea on Pluto, 'n' caught a kiwi crony yawn.

     Near you, saucy mate, ten agate trays knee us, says us.

Near you sag lie ace who you scar up. Poi oat an auk toss.

Near you, so's Cal, list-tossin' air hoop. O Ilion, ail thee.

Tone all 'lone Danny own, met Tom, moo moan appeal lay on a

Allah lap pad knows sayin'. Pow! Roast day! High ape petal louse.

     Hide are Annie's urine takin' crap. Atone, take a son, tea.

Guy cone Europe! Ooh, low! You Polly Nessus tackle lewdness.

Tuna, oop! Oedipus Tech high on tea. Pause. Hey, gay's ass ta'en.

The salary? He'd woe Heraclid Tao when act toes.

Thursday trick onto (Glop! Foo!) rye, 'n' aces tick who on toe.

     Noon out whose so-so wheat top pale ass geek cone Argos 'n' I own

Height alone height a lopin' height at Trachis an amount to

Height takin' Phthia. Aid Hellas, call Lee 'goon,' Ike. Ah!

Moor mead, honest day Cal lay unto Gay Helen is Guy Achaioi.

Tone now Pentagon tan! Neon in our Cossack: kill, lay us.

Alloy goop, pull 'em. Aye, you do say 'chaos,' 'semen.' No! On toe!

Ooh, Gary knows 'tis spin a piece. 'Stick us,' say gays. I, too.

Kay to Gary? Nay, a sip o' darkies. D' you sack? He'll lay us.

Co-risk, O men, nose Brie. Say he does say you come. I you?

Ten-neck learn his swag, sell Leto? Pole llama gay sauce!

Lure Ness undie, abort. They saw sky take ya, Thebes.

Goddamn moon ate Abel. Link I a piss strophe awning & seem morose?

Huey ass you annoy. Oh sail, ape. Pee on a Tao, an' act toes.

Teas, O gay Kate tacky, on tack odd Ann stays, says 'thigh am melon.'

     Hide ache on fool lock ink hyper ration. Anthem: Moe went 'Ta.'

Demeter, us tame men, us eat tone, not tame meat tear a melon.

Ankh, he alone Tantra owe nigh dip, tell Leon lick a boy in.

Tow now pro Tessie louse. Array you. Say game on you, eh?

Zoo's eon tote a day, day a Ken caught a guy. Ah! My liner!

Today Guy am feed rupees, a low cusp fool Locke. Kay yell 'A late toe!'

Guide a mossy middle, a stone decked on a Tartan nose. Sun, air!

Nay, us a pot rose gone to Polly Protest on a guy own.

Ooh dame an' ooh die a narc, oh yes, an' pot thee on gay men, narc cone.
Allah, spay us! 'Cause mace epode arc ace! So's dose hairy O's.
If a gluey Oz pole loom may loop fool lock, kid Dao!
Ow! Toke a signet toes. Make a tomb moo. Protest ill. Ow!
Hope low Tarots gain a Yoda. Map wrote 'Tarots sky airy own.'
Heroes' pro, Tessie Louse, array us suited 'til ahoy.
D' you want they game on nose Poe? They own gay men, nestle on neon. ('Ta!)
Totem mat is a'rockin', Tommy. Line nine, Aesop on toe.
        Hide, defer ass, 'n' aim onto Pa. Ripe boy bay eat a limb, neighin'.
Boy bane Guy clap fear a sky uked team inane, Iolchos.
Tone irk? Admit toy you feel asp. High syndic Annie own.
You male lost, own up, admit oat, take Eddie a goon ikon.
Alcestis, peel ya? Oh, two? Got Ron aid, dose a wrist, eh?
        Oy! Dare ram mate horning eye, thou mock yen, inner moan toe!
Guy Meliboee neckin' gay you list. On it, Ray. Kay yawn.
Tone day? Philoctetes' air can! Toke's own, you aid does.
Hip to neon? Harry tighten heck as tippin' takin'. 'Ta!
Em, babe, Hassan took son you aid. Otis syph he mock, kiss thigh.
Hollow men any soak ate toke rot. Here all gay, ya pass cone.
Lemnos in egg at the yea! Haughty mean leapin', we, yes, a guy own.
Hell, Kay! Mock these? Don't talk cock oil loop! Pro knows who drew.
In toga Kay tacky on talk. A dame (nay!) says thigh a melon.
Are gay? (Yoip!) Are a new? See Phil lock tit (ow!) an' knock toes.
Ooh, de men nude! Doyenne are coy, ace on potty. On gay men are cone.
Allah maid dunk 'cause Mason oil lay us, know those who wee us.
Tone Rhett takin'! Rainy hoop oil leap tall, leap o'er toe.
Hide day cunt, trick Cain! Guy? He, though mean, Chloe mock Coe, his son.
High takin' I collie in pole, in you' root, too. I call Leah, us.
Tune out 'Hey, gay, stay,' 'n' Asclepius do (oh?) pie day.
Yet Terah got to puddle air. You said Dame Mock cow own.
Tease debt tree ache on tag, laugher! Wry 'nay' zesty co-own, too.
        Hide achin', or many on high tea cranin', Hyperion!
Height take on ass, tear yond tit on 'No!' You tell Luke, 'Cock arena.'
Tone air cure (oop!) pool (us you I). Mono sag louse (swee' us).
Toad ham? Attis are rock. Hunt 'em, Mel, I nigh. Nay, yes, sip on toe.
        Hide our geese on a cone, Guy. Curtain nanny moan, too.
Or Thane ail, loan in tape all in tall low sauna Luke cane.

Tune out hegemony, Women! Hip Ptolemy spool loop-boy Tess.
We us Perithoos, ton at Hannah toast take a toe, Zeus.
Tone row Pope Perry tote 'take-a-toke' Lou. Toss hip ode. Ah, may ya!
Aim at it, toe tea. Fear as settees sat toll. Lock neigh ain't us.
Two-steak Pelion hose a guy. High, thick, is he, pale Lassen.
Ooh, coy, oh Sam! Motto, gay Leontes! So's dose sorry O's.
Who, you? Super theme, O Yoko! Row nuke? I need Tao!
Toys, Dom. At Escher a cunt (ah!) may lie nigh. Nay, yes, a pun too.
      Goon eh? Us stake coop who egg gay Duo, Guy ache. Oh sea (nay!) ass!
Toy Denny any sip onto men hip Ptolemy tape a wry boy.
High pair read Dodona. Induce gay mare. Ron high key attend to.
High Tom pee mare ton tit hairy so ne'er gain a man, too.
Hose Rae's Peneus. Pro (yes!) call Lear, rowin' nuder.
Ooh! Do gay pain. Nay, oh soon Miss Gay tie our gear row tinny.
Allah tame, mean cat, hooper, then hep, peer Rae, eh Ute? Tell lie, own.
Or cougar deign noose. Styx who'd dot toe cyst in a poor oaks.
      Magnet on dare keep rot house ten thread dawn nose, swee' us.
Hoy Perry pain neon guy, peel Leon, eh? Knows he peel lone?
Nah! Yes, cone! Tone men pro those those hey gay man new, eh?
T' ode Dama, Tess, Sarah conned a male line. Eye nay us, hip on toe.
      Hoot toy are hegemony, Stan (noun). Guy coy, Ra annoy, ace sawn.
Tease Tartan auk. A wrist tossin' Sumo yen. Nape pee, Muse saw.
Ought Tony dip pone? I am a trade daisy nip on toe.
Hip boy men make. A wrist tie us on fairy tea, add Tao.
Tass, you may lose élan. Epode: do Kay ass sore knit as hose?
Oh trick us, soy. Yet tea us, strap fully apin' no Tony sauce.
Tass sayin' Perrier trips our guru, tokes. So's Apollo.
Am foot to lay us, foe bone? Array us for uses.
And Ron now make a wrist toss, sayin' 'Tell a moan, knee us, sigh yes.'
'Offer Achilles many in hogar, Polly,' fair tot toes sayin'.
Hip boy toy porous cone. Amy moan, appeal: 'Lay on.' (Nah!)
Hello, men. Any S see Corot knee sip onto poor Roy's sea?
Kite a pome, me knees, as Agamemnon knee poem many lie on.
A trade: 'Hail a high day.' 'Pa Ra rake many,' the lass says.
'Disco is sinter pond,' toke I. 'I gonna ace in yentes.'
Toke soy sin, the hip boy day. Pa Ra, arm moss. In high sin Heck cost toes.
Low tone? A rep too many? Hell, you tripped on tessile linen!

Hesta-San arm at a 'D'you pep pookahs' men?' Nah! Kate towin' hocked tone.
Ink lease, yes? Hide archon, array if Phil on pot. The un-Tess!
Fight on in tacky in tack at ass Stratton who deem mock cunt toe.
   Hide our reason, nosy. Tape who reek thump as son name I too.
Gaia dupe pest. Tenor keys Daddy-O's. Tear 'pick' around 'know.'
Combing no tit, tamp pit tufu. Weigh guy, Annie Massey.
In a rim ice hot. Tip us, sit tough foe. You semen eye, Eunice.
Hose a rat on a Pope. Posse make a stain. Knock keys debt, O Gaia.
Air comin' on. Mallet oak cad. Dieppe praisin' paid yo-yo.
   Trojans dangle, assail the pod: 'Danny must soak a, uh, Iris.'
'Party us,' sigh Iggy. 'Oh coy you!' Soon angle Yale leggy, nay?
Hide agora sag, gory you own ape peep Priam owe. You too racy?
Panties some may gay raise, same men, you (yea!) dig Aaron, teas.
Ankh! Who'd hissed the many prose syph hip ode as o.k., a Iris?
'Ace,' said a diphthong in 'Who-ye-Priam.' Oh you polite tea!
Host tow owns couple, sees day buttock. Ace seep a boy, toss
Tomb boy a pack rot. Tot wise, wait, augur on toes.
Dig men as hobo, ten now. Pinafore meet they in Achaioi.
Toy Minnie ace a many prosy fee pod as (o.k!) a Iris.
"O Gay Ron, I ate toy myth, I acrid toy ace scene.
Hose Poe. Oh to pay rainy spool, lay most all Leah's toes a'roaring.
Emend 'dame.' Allah appall Lama, cusses 'Salute Onan, drone!'
All loophole tyin' debt to Sunday tale (ow!) no pauper.
Lee anger foolish scene (yoik!). Oh to sip Sam, math icing!
Irkin' type Eddie yo-yo mock Esau. Many pro tea as two.
Hector side dame, maul list. Tepid hello, my ode. Dead dare wreck sigh.
Paul like ark cat, ass tomb make gap Priam whip peccary.
All aid alone glows sop. Oh loose pair rayon and trope own.
Toy scene, heck! Cost us an Air. Say 'mine,' 'het.' Wise sip a rare Kay.
Tone deck say 'Gay stoke 'cause mess salmon-nose Polly ate us.'"
   Hosephat! Hector duty the Ossip, pose egg: no yes Zen.
Hype sod loose sog or rain nape pit U.K. Add essay, want to.
Pa side wig new, 'n' to pool I ached days. Who toll, Laos?
Paste I th' hippies, tap all us store-room mocked us so roar, Rae.
   A steed day? 'Tis proper, right. Tap all Ios, I pay a Colony.
Impede you' weapon, youth. Ape pair he'd roam. Us in tacky enter.
Tinny toy Andrews bat, yea! Yankee Clay's cousin.

At Hannah toy debt a same apple hose cart. My oh Marine ace!
In that total Troy? Yes! Steady ache written Oedip-peek: 'Ooh, Roy!'
     Trojan many game on new whim. May gas core a thigh o' loose Hector?
Priam me days, ha! Model gay Polly plays toy. Guy a wrist toy.
Light Tories on tomb, maim out his ink, a yea sea.
     Dardanian now Turkey. New spies, Anchises.
Aeneas, stone hoop Anchises' tech kiddie, Aphrodite.
Edie's sinkin' 'em, my sea. Thea brought tow unit ace saw.
'Ook! I us!' am motto. Gay duo (Aunt, Tenor) rose (who? yea!).
Arkie low cost talk a mass tame mock. 'Kiss you, aide, dote ape,' us says.
     I dazzle Leon an' I un-hoop pipe ode. Any auto need ace?
Often neigh I pee known: 'Tess Sue, dormez lawn?' I say 'Boy, ho!'
Trow us stone out here. Kill Lou cow, no-sag louse (whee!) us.
Pander us, O Guy. Toke son Apollo now. Toes Edo can.
Hide Dad, race stay on take. Conk I, demon. Up ice, Sue.
Cape pit way on achin' guy. Tear Ra's sore rose, I poo.
Tone air cadre stows take. I am amphi-hustlin'? Note whore acts.
'We aid woe.' Mare rope, pose spur, cuss you, hose, pay rip, pant on.
Hey, Damon tossin' us, odious pied ass say us gay.
Stay Cain as pole lemon if tease a Nora toad, eh? Oh you tea!
Pay the stain. Care Rae's scar raggin' melon nose than at 'Hojo'?
     Hide our wrapper coat. Ink I, proct yon amp pain name moan to.
Guy Sestos 'n' Guy Abydos neck on Guy Dionne. Airy Spain!
Tune out tour, tacky days. Sir Cassius sore. Come, us sand Ron
As you, Sir Tacky Days, on a respite tempera, nip poi,
Heighten ass, make a leap at a moo up a silly yen: toes.
     Hippo those, dog. A pool, a pale lass goin' ink, kiss a moron.
Tone high? Larissa an air rib, bollock an eye, yet ass scone.
Tone irk? Hip boat host appeal lie. You stows dose, array O's.
We ate due woe. Late, though, you pale us, goo. T' you, Tommy Dao.
     Out art! Rake Cossack, gawk a mast. I pare rosy rows.
'Oh sue us, Hellespont! Oh saga!,' Rose sent to Sergei.
     Euphemous dark husk eco-known. In ache mate town.
We owes Troezen, know Yod, Dio. Trap fey husk, ya Dao.
     Out tarp poor Reich may sag a pie on as sang cool low tokes. Whose?
Tale loathin' hex a mood, own us a pox. Your worry: rayon toes.
Axe you who call his tone nude! Or a peak kid not I eye on.

Paphlagonians dig gay toe pool, lemony us! Lassie on care.
Ex-Senate owner, then Hemi-Onan, gay, knows a grot Terah own.
High rocky torah-neck conk I. Say 'salmon am.' Pen name: 'Moan Toe.'
Armpit apart in yond pot o' moan glued automat an eye on
Chrome non-Thai key alone take I hoop sail loose air root in noose.
    Out are alleys, dough known, odious sky, a pea's trope, a Serkin.
Tell loathin' necks a lube bass hot tenor guru west tea gain net lay.
    Muse on deck, roam his air cake eyeing no mo' soy yoni's stays.
All look coy on Noyes' sin. Nehru sought a caramel lie, Nan.
Allah'd a May hoop poker, sip, pod door k.o.'s Aeacides.
In pot Tom — oh ho — the pert Trojans care. Rice day, guy all loose.
    Fork us, sow! Frug gas say 'Gay guy ask canny us the O, aid days.'
Telex ask canny ace 'Maim a Sandy's mini-mock, kiss thigh.'
    Mayo's scene now messed laced guy, Auntie Foe say gays saw us stain.
Who yet tall limey neigh a stogie? Guy yet take a leman, eh?
Hike I may own. As egg gone hoop pot, mole-low gay gout toss.
    Nasty sow car own, hey gay sought a barber. Oh phone on!
High Miletus! Neck hump thee, runt Taurus sock, read (awful!) on.
My end root tear, row ass. Shmoo call his Taipei knocker 'Reina.'
Towin' men are amphi-mock, hose guy. Nasty say gay sauce stain.
Nasty Sam pee mock hose, stain no Om. Me, O Nose, saw Glaa tech. (Nah!)
Hose guy cruising a cone, pull 'em undie in a Ooh! Take who Rae.
Nape you, Sue! Dirty high toga pair kiss, sell Lou, groan hole, ate Ron.
All laid, damn may (oop!) poke air. See Poe dough chaos, sigh 'Ah,' kid Tao.
In Poe, Tom (oik!) cruise on dock, kill, lay us seco (Miss said die if frown).
    Sarpedon dare Ken, look you. Guy glow 'cause a moo moan —
Tale o' ten-neck Luke kiosks and two uppity neighin' toes.

Phaestos/Matala
May 29, 1983

BOOK III

Off t' Araby! 'cause me th' henna *amie*. Ye moan a cynic Oz tea.
Trojan men clang eating no peat, tisane Norn 'neath Hess hose.
Eat tape. Bear clawing ye yare, a known pale lure, a know thee pro.
Eight tape you 'n' he moan, a fig gone gay. Athos fatten numb brawn.
Clang! Ye eat a (yea!) pedant, ape, o.k. a neo-roe Ah own.
'Un-thrash he pig may easy phoning gay gear,' a fair ruse say.
Ye airy Ed, the rot, eh? Yer cock keen ne'er read the prof her undy.
Heed dull reason. See ye many up knee owned us. A 'hey, ye'
In thee, Moe, my mouth tas' a lick semen alley leasin'.

    After you score reef easy, know Tosca tech heaven, O me clean
Pea messy new tip feel lean, clapped teat that unique toss amino.
Toss ode: 'Tea step pea love sea.' O son, tap heel on knee scene.
Oh Sarah, toney Pope us seek on knees, all low sore, neat Thai lease.
Heir comin', known mallet. Though cud ye, ape reason pay the eel.

    He doted, he skid on niece, on a pal Lily see. Knee yawn days.
Truss sin, men. Pearl my keys in a lake sand throes, they'll weed th' ease.
Pard the lain. Oh me! Cynic own quai, calm pee Lotto suck.
Cake syph fuss sow tarot, though ready oak ache or wreath men a hall coal.
Pal loan are ye own pro call lizard, oh pawn. Tass arrest us
On TV, own mock his ass. They in an idiot eat he.

    Tone those soon in. We sin are, if Phil us. Men a louse.
Ere Homer (non-pro Pa) wreathin' nummy, loom mock her a 'vive' on Da.
Oh stay, lay own! A hareem, a gal, lo, it be so, Medicare sauce!
Afro kneel a funky round knee, agree own egg. Gaah!
Pee noun Moloch art take a test: Three ye pare enough tone.
'Seven day to haze steak,' 'keen is the lair,' read Daisy.
Oh suck a ream men, a louse! Alex and drone, they weed ya.
Of th' alm ease scene, knee, though own fought toga art tease, us they
        all eat teen
'Oft teak add decks suck young scene tough kissin' alto ham,' Oz say.

    Tone, though soon in Noe sin Alec-San (th't) us the Wheaties.
Imp, Rome, a he see fun 'n' Doc cut tip plea ye feel lone, neat or
Up stood our own knees, sith know (say) has a toke key Raleigh known.
Us, though titties, tether a cone dyed own pal lean, whoreson a pesty
'Ooh, Ray us.' Envy, cease seep at row muscle. Ave, ye, uh . . .
Up, Stan, a whore he sen'. Oh gross! Stem in eely Perry, us!

Oh soft ease: cot, a meal, an Eddy of Trojans. Hire rogue, hon'.
These awes ought Ray us eon all Exxon dross they weed (these?).
　　　　Dunned thick turn knee kiss. An' he don' ask 'Greece epicene?'
"These spar reed those arrest (eh?) ye. Name a Nessie pair up Bev. (Ta!)
Ethyl fellas sag on us, Tim. Men neigh. Aga must topple 'less they
Kick it. A bully mean kickin' Polly. Care thee, onion,
You toe-loving dame in neck ape, up seein' alone.
He Pooh, Kung hollow. Oh seek, carry comb. Oh own Tess. Come, won't
　　　　us a hay?
Fondest are wrist tea, a promo anemone eunuch, cock alone.
Either say Paul Lucas (TV), a phrase sin, nude that tease alky.
Eaty O's. They Onan pond, oh pour Rhee's in a sea.
Punt on a pip low sauce, set a rosary ear as I ye razz.
Meek these a loathe happy sea ye neck heavy they a knee? Yes!
Ex-happy ease, yea! Ease neon Nan throwin' (Ech!) meat Ah own!
Pat Reed is some mega-pee mop pole, eat a bandida thee mo'?
These men is sin men. Harm mock at ye, fiend. Thus ye oft do.
Ook! On thee, meanie, Ah's sorry ye feel on men allowin'.
Knee ease he you. Photos say he's taller in parakeet teen
Who candy craze. Mickey the wrist at tether. Rough road it is.
Eat tickle meat. Tote aid those so ten can knee ye, seamy ye! (Ease!)
Allah, Ma, lot row aesthete thee. Moan a sea, take a knee, thee
Lyin' honest so he tone a cock. Onan? Ech! Oh sigh your 'Gaahs.'"
　　　　Toned of tape prose ape pen a lake sand throes. Theo weed these.
"Hector rape pea, make cot, ace on any case. A sooty Paris sun.
Eighty craw the ye. Pay, lay key (so says Tina) at ear ease.
Hostage India thorough seep on arrow. So's rotted (ech!) knee.
Knee con neck t' Omni. Seen a felly? Then throws arrow, wean.
Oh see any's teeth, as 'Sin not,' 'tar vetos.' Know 'oh' says tea.
Mimi, though rare, a top row fare (ech!) resay 'Ease sof' row thee tease.'
Ooh! Tea above lea taste teeth they own. Eric key they awe, though Ra.
O suckin' off teat, though. Sin neck own th' (ooh!) Cannes tease, elite toe.
Kneein' of team meth, Alice ball 'em easy, knee them a kiss. They
All loose men. Kathy's under (oh?) husky pandas. A 'hey, youse!'
Oft are a men mess soak, carry feelin' men allow, own.
Seem valet Tom fell. Lenny cake team. Us see *passim* a hiss. They
(Oh butter roast) thicken knee. Keys agree, sewin' to ya neater.

Team mother low neigh panda. Your neck got ache. Other yeas, though.
Eee! The leafy Lotte tackier key ya piece. Starter moan, Tess.
Nay eat. Ate tree. He never like her teethin' his thong.
Our guess is: 'sip of a donkey,' 'a hay eater,' 'collie.' 'Ye neck her!'"
     Oh syph it! Heck, tore it off, tickle ream, egg gummy, though knock
         goo sauce.
Care us messin' yond roe Onan. Nay airy, if along us
May sooth, ooh! Rose alone teethe either, e'en thee, sauna, upon Dis.
Toe they pet talks Oz, owned duck. A Rico moaned as Achaeans.
Easin' debt, it tease scum, any lice seat Tev alone.
Oft aroma, crone a easin' a' knocks on throne naug 'em Mame known.
"Is Hess the 'are-ye-me' volley tech? Ooh, Rhea hay own!
'S Dave. Take our tea, oppose a Rae ink or wreath Thea low sector."
     Oh syph o' thee. Thus Hun dumb a he sawin'. Nay, oat, eh? Yea!
        Known doe
Is semen nose. Hector the mate Tom fought. Terry's sin nape pay.
"Cackle eat tame after whisk gay. Eek! Knee me the suck hay.
Myth on a lick, son. Three ought to wean neckin'. Eek! Us a'roarin'.
All loose men callet ate roe. Ask gay pond! Us a 'hey youse.'
Dove 'hey' a call up at this 'they,' a peak, though nipple Eve. (Oh teary!)
Oft tone then mess soak gay are reef, feel lone men allowin'.
Use 'some fell on knee,' 'cake tea Ma sip us,' 'seem Ma kiss they.'
Up poet to Rose: 'The Kenny key sea craze Sunday.' Ya neat, eh?
Cut team, math alone neigh. Panda ye naked. Take other yes, though.
He, Dolly, feel low. Teat talk gay orc. Ya pieced tot, a moment."
     Oh syph o' thee, thereupon dey sockin': 'Nay, yea! None dose ye up. Pee!'
Tease, seethe, the gay mate a ape of a wean. Ugh! O' those men a louse!
"Cackly ten, e'en gay *amie*. O'Malley stagger, Al go seek a knee.
Theme moan name moan fro, nay, ho, the 'thee' a green theme in (nay!) thee.
Odd ye use Kate, row us a peacock. A Paul lap pep us. They,
Ena, came. Ease serried those gay Al licks. Sand ruin Neckar keys.
He moan, though, Po tear wroth on a toss. Come 'ere, rot. A teaked, eh?
Death nail ye, all Lethe. Thee a greened heat, a talky star.
Ease city are at her own laugh cone, eh? Tear e'en them, allay Nan.
Ye take a 'ye,' Eli? Oh 'thee thee' me cease. Some men all lone.
Ox set a 'they ape Rhea.' Me of ye enough roar key at Omni.
Aft toss a pea ye pay. The sea pear feel leak. Gay appease tea.

Meaty sea pear vase see ye. Thee, oh sore key, o' thee lease eat, eh?
Eh? Though plot, her own on-throne frenzy air wrath on Day.
Ease, though, your own Met. A ease in a map rose so gay appease, so
Love sea oppose so. Car east, Tom mate Tom. Foe tear ease sea. (Yeh,
    neat, eh?)"
    Oh suffer thee the hair ease, son. A hay eat ate row, Estée.
Ail pome. Many puff sauce they (oh?) easy rue. Roll 'em (me, you):
Carry Pooh's manner. Eek, son! A piece stick us *sec*. The Yvonne of tea.
Tough hay at Tex sat the un-dote. Amen gotta (then) tape ye gay. Ye
Please see an Ali lone. Aw, Lee, ye thee numb. Fees are rural.
Hectored ape rôti, a steed. Thee, Okie, reek. Ah, sip Ebbe!
Carpal limos are nasty. Fair in pre-Ammon tickle less say.
Oft are a tall thieve Ian pro ye (eek!) re-own, a (Gaa!) maim known.
Knee us a pig laugh he Ross seein' (nay, thar) nickle leaven.
Sis semen nail the rook cop pee, thee sog. A Mame known knee thee (oh!).
    Eerie's thaw of the layin' eel lef' colon know wan yellow. Seal, then,
Edom any gallow oh wan teen know wreathe thou the mart tea.
Teen on teen? Or wreathe these sea-cake re-own Nelly cow own?
Lao thee keen pre-*amie*. Oh, thee got roan? Neither sari's teen.
Teen th' ever in Meg. Arrow we them. Agony stony fen, eh?
Thee, Plaka porphyry, e'en Paul lay us, then ape, ass. Pass an eye, th' loose
Trow on thee, Poe. The moan gay a hay own hall. Co-heat tone known.
Ooh, Seth! Any neck? Ape? Ass? *Honi* par Rio's pal o' my own.
On who these Tamany prose say fee Poe thus soak gay I eerie's?
"They've wreath. E'en knee 'em, Fa. Feelie, e'en a (the) scale lyre guide the A.
Trow own thee Poe. (The moan gay a hay own.) Hulk co-heat tone known.
Heap preen Nepal lily sea. Pharaoh pole lea the greener Rhea.
In bed the (oh, oh) low we owe. Ol' he lay o' ma' knee, Pauly, me O!
Heed thee? Knee, nay? Ah Tess see ye. Paul lay most they pep oft, eh?
As speedy, cackly men knee Pa, Roth then (hey!) amok wrapup peein'.
Oft are a lake sand throes scary feel lows men allow us.
Mock reason, he easy seem. A he, Sunday Perry, see you.
Toe the Kenny key. Sandy fee (eek!) ache. Lease see ya, key tease."
    Oh see, Pooh saw they a glee keen knee. Mare own 'em (valley
    theme, Moe).
And: Thrush stay, pro tear rook, eh? (Ah, stay!) Oh seethe, they took ye on.
Oft teak other yen knees. Sickle leaps some men neo, though knee scene

Or Ma taketh all o' me. Oh! Terra 'n' cotta thuck Greek, eh? (Oh, ça!)
Ooh, key ye, Amati. (Yea! Kay amphi-Hyppolyte thee a pawn doe,
A the.) Repeat: 'Thee us thee got Turk,' 'Gleam many Dave,' 'Oh, oh! Peace!'
Hypes sad the pithy cannon know these cape peel. Lay ease, son.

    Heed thumb fee pre-almond gape on, though knee they theme
            meat team.

Lamb bone take cleat he own. Thee Kate. Town a tow zone Ari owes.
Ooh, call leg owned. A gay auntie, nor pep knee men. Wham, foe!
He ought to thee mow. Yer own days say 'Peace gay easy, peel easy.'
Ye writhe? Thee, Paul, lay me, oh pep of many, y'all log gore eat, eh?
Ace th' lea titty yes, seein' naked Tessie take Kathy lean.
Then th' rail affects Khomeni. Oh Pa, leery Wes sonny easy.
Tea ye a rot row *honi* ye tore us in day pee peer go.
He, though soon, 'neath (own) the Lenin a peeper gon' you, son.
Eek! Up Rosalie loose, eh? Pay. Apt tear went 'Ah go ravin'.'
"Ooh nemesis name assist, row us gay. Eek! Knee me thus a hay ooze.
Teethe thumb fee ye neck keep Paul lean groanin'. All (yea!) a pause keen.
Anus saw th' honnête tease seethe. They's Aesop, Pa achin'.
Allah gay oh steep airy use any. Ya seen Ace, though?
Me thee mean take a ass seat top. Piece soapy Molly pee toe."
Oh sorry, fan, Priam most the Léonie necklace sot toe phony.
"They've rope a wreath they'll th' ooze a feel lone, take us ease (of a me you)
Off writhe these brought her own. Day pose scene peel. Stay feel loose stay.
Ooh, Timmy et ye. As seethe they knee me yet t' ye ease scene.
Eee! Me a form ease, son. Paul lay moan Paul lead the green (nah!) hay own.
Awesome meek gay tone than th' raw pay lorry on Exxon a meanies.
Hostess sew this Tina (hey!). Oh son, near ye stay Meg, us stay.
Eat team, men gay, fall. Leak Emmy's zone. Folly nestle Leah. Ah, sea!
Gallon th' ooh. Toe ego new po' we, though 'nuff. (Th' all missing.)
Ooh, Thu toy a rawer own vase seal league around three ache-y."

    Tone the layin' knee myth thee see nummy vet. Oh thee, I ye neck own.
"Adios, stemmy! Yes, if feel Lake Ear-Red, thee nose stay.
Oh Sophie lend the the knot toes. Me a thee 'n' cock hose sop pâté.
    They've roe!
Yayy! So a pome mean! Th' all, among no twos! Tell lip 'Oh, ça!'
Pay that ate eely yeti 'n' gay yummy leakin' era teen kneein'.
Allah tag gook, eh? Ye known doe toke gay clay you sought, a teak. Ah!

Toot owe the tea airy. Oh oh, Ma knee Rae, the metal lass.
Ooh Tosca trade these a freak Creon nog a maim known.
Alm foe, tear own vassal if stagger th' husk rot hero's steak meaty's.
Th' era of tame Moses a key (no pee?). Those seep hôte ta'en ya."
    O's fat, oh tone, though (yeh!) roe knee gas a toe phony send Day.
"Om mock a rot trade thee Midi yen Ace soul of you they moan.
Eee! Ronny tipple, Edith me yacht occur ya (hey!) own.
Eee! The gay free. E'en easy Lethe own a bellow Wace, son.
Ain't thigh, though!, 'n' pleased twos free us on era's sail low Paul lose.
Louse sought tree us gay MiG, though nose Sadhi they you,
Erato test rot own dope are rook the song 'Ari He You.'
Kay gotta go. Nay, peek who Rose sayin' mate a tease scene, a lick thee 'n'
He might tote, ate eel, though nummy zone is undy a near Rae.
Allude t' thee? Toss ye son a seal, leak go. Peace, Achaioi!"
    They've tear enough to th' easy eye, though nary in (oy!) airy us
"Seep I (ye). Meek gay tone the feelin' take us so 's tease, so this tea
Me own men carefully. Nag, gum 'em known nose sot très ye (thou)
Every terrace, though me sin, need the starin' Nisei knee. Thus they
Tough (hey!) a many-keyed epic, though knee pool leave votary.
Oft toe's thick teal low: 'Peep-hole eat ace,' 'stick us and their own.'
Are neo-mean a go gay scope? Yes, seem mellow.
Osteo 'n' mega-poi thee heir hate a 'are yen noun.'"
    Tone thee, me vet a pee. The lane either you *sec* (yayy!) off he o-
"Ut tossed off liar tea o' these Pauly meat tease so these safes.
'Ostrophe ain't thee. Moe eat a kiss, craw Anaïs pair use cease.
He, though, spun tea use, Ted, though loose gamey they a peek? Nah!"
    Teen th' oft undy nor pep knee menace undy. Oh knee the
"O ye name a lot two-toe oppose knee 'em. Erté say 'pace.'
Eee! Thee God gay! They've rowboat eely. The thee (us) o' thee save us.
Save a neck Cannes, yell 'Lee, ease sinner reef feel low men allow.'
Two's thug waxin' niece suck gay in me g'reasy feel Lisa
Am. Foe tear o'en they. Feein' a thigh 'n' gay media pique? (Nah!)
Alló, Ted. Thee t' row a scene in a 'grow many scene,' a meek then
Stand. Own men, Menelaus. Seep peer a hen. Every us a moose.
Ah 'm foe, they's omen know you're a rotor-rose see 'n' know thee save us.
Alló, Ted, thee myth, whose gamey they a paw sin knee, feign knowin'.
Eat teemin' men allows a peat row, ha! Thee 'n' Ah go rave, eh?

Paw of raw men a law maw loll (yea). Oh say pee you pull Lee, me thus.
Ooh, the off a mar to whip piece sea gay 'n' knee hystero seein'.
Alló Ted thee, Paul, Lee me teasin', Ike see 'n' know thee save us.
"'S task, Kenny pay, they this gay got (Ach!), though know (oh?) Ma top peaks us.
Skipped done th' (ooh!) toe pee. Sew tip, pro preen. Ace enema?
Allah stem fizz (ech!). A skin neither Rae fought ye-ache-us
Face, 'cause a coating titty nay men, eh, Afro-naut tuft toss?
Alló to thee, up atom egg a lean necks teeth they us see, Eee!
Kay pay honey father scene, eh? Caught a he, merry ease scene.
Ooh! Can a pee toe these? These say 'yeh'! Airy sea ever wrote to Saul, us?
'Ooh' taught ago, though thee see ol' saga. Some meth? Thee those
            sea-thunders."
        Toe tree ton of ta'en dye, though ne'er ain' O ureas.
"Tease tarot th' Allah's all hail's an eerie east Emmy gusty.
Exodus, are ye uncle folly 'n' take a every us, oh moose?"
        Tone the Lenny tawny. Pep loss? Amoeba! To thee a ye neck owin'.
"Ooh toss they us ass tip, a low real circus suck (hey!) own.
Idomeneus that arrow then ninny Crete a seethe they o' sauce.
As stick comfy the mean Cretan nag ye (ya wraith, hon?) day
Paul lucky minx scene knees. Sane are ye if feel loss. Men knell louse.
Eek! Owe any mate arrow up at ache? Re-teethe any key toe?
Kneein' the loose men, pandas sorrow a lick. Go pus, Achaians.
Ooh skinny eke knee in Gate Two. No, ma'am, myth he say mean.
The oath dude thee? Nah! May they Inca's meat tore ale Ah own.
Castor wrath heap o' the moan. Gay peek's saga thong Pauly they've caw.
Oft toke a cygnet, Toto. Mimi a ye 'n' atom meat tear.
You hasp, pest thin lock Ed. They moan us sex Sarah teenies.
Eee! They've room an' upon données say 'Knee pond over easy.'
Kneein' oft, Duke Ethel lose sea mock ink at a theme: Many on throne.
Ace hay o' thee? Thee ought Tess gay on knee. They up all o' me yes teen."
        Oh Spot Toe! Two's 'Thee, thee.' Caught a hen feces? Oh? Say 'Ah.'
In locker they moan (yow!) 'thief.' Feel Lee, 'n' pot wreathe thee, gay.
        Kiri kiss than nasty. They own Pharaoh, nor key appease Da.
Odd nay thee, oh gay known. Nay, if Ron a carp pone, a Ruhr ease.
Us goin' neigh. Ye offer a they-critter: rough fine known.
Key reek, seethe they, us see they hurry, see yucky Pale law
Haute treein' in their under-Paris. Tom 'n' us up a Essene.

"Or sail Lao may th' undie Ah thee call lay you seen a wrist tea.
Truant thee Poe the moan gay Achaian hall. Cohere tone own.
Is sped thee own caught of inane orc? Ye a piece taught 'dammit,' eh?
Oft are alike: Son throws gayer he if he loves men allows.
Mocker ease in he easy, Ma, he son dumb feel ye necky.
Toe they Kenny key Sunday ye knee gay ache Timothy, Peto.
Eat the leaf, feel it, eat a gay or key a piece taught Tom Mondays.
Neal meant 'tree inner evil.' A cut teeth, then neigh on Day.
Argos says hippo vote on gay a 'Hey ye the collar ye neck caw!'"

Hose fat, or he ye send, though your own neck élève say the tear ruse.
'Heap puce,' Zev gunny manatee thought. 'Rally us up, pith on doe.'
On therapy, Priam us caught a thee knee, a teen in a piece sow.
Paw, are they on tea? Nor Perry call, lay a V-set. Oh thief, Ron.

To they the ass gay 'n' pay thee, own the hon. O.k. a sip who's
All low to thee. Rico 'n' dumb mate at roe ask gay a 'hey, youse.'
Ex-sea pawn apple. Von Day say pique, though Napoli vote tea, Ron.
Ace meson Trojan gay a hay, oh Nestea! Hoe onto
Horny toad th' off t' eke a peter an ox sunned row knock 'em, maim known.
And though thee saves Polly meat tease, sot are key reek kiss, sog. Ave!
Or key a piss tot. They own synagogue, greet teary they (ye) known.
Miss Gonad tar vase sea, lives scene. Knee, though rape. He hear us,
        O Heaven!
Ah tray these their ease, some on us. He race sea my hair on
Eee! Ye parks if fey us make a cool Leon neighin' Artaud.
Are known neck if a' layin' Tom? Nate trick us after a peter.
Key reek Castro own gay (a hay own) knee manner, wrist tease.
Teasin' thought re: These make a lef het a he, a son ass hone.
"Zev putter. Wreathe thee then. 'Meth,' they yawn. Key these tame (may
        ye stay).
Eely us those punned if for us gay pond to Pa coo wheeze.
Gay pawed Tom, me keg gay, a cape unearth the common Da's.
Anthro Pooh's teenies, though notice képi orgone Nome mos' see.
Eee! Me smart, teariest. If feel loss at tether key, appease Da.
He Mencken men allowin' all licks on the rose caught up. If knee
Oft toss a pee, the Lenin Hecate toe cake team ought to pawn Da.
He miss th' any Essene neigh? Oh meth, a punned up a reason.
Eee! The calyx and wrong teen. Eck! Sawin' those men a louse.

Trojans a pcc th' Helen kneein' cake team at a pond up oath who neigh.
Team mean thar' ye ease. Sup o' teen, namin' kneein' teen, nay ye can
Eat tech kiss o' me knees. See mate on throw peas, see pale eat, eh?
Eee! The nummy team mean, Priam! Paree am me oh tape o' this
Teeny nuke Ethel low scene Alex on three you piss sewn dose.
Aft are ago képi, Tom. A he sew? May neck a penis?
Off theme men known knee us kettle us pull 'em. Me auk (hee, hee!), yo."
        Eek! Kay a post. Om. A Hussar known to many lay Hulk Coe.
Kate ooze men. Caught a thickener peek, though nose sauce spare
        owned us.
Theme moot, they've omen noose up Hoag, arm men. Know seal it? Toe
        hulk cuss.
E'en none th' accrete tea rose a fee summon. Knee the Pa, Ace sin.
A Kay *honi* they've Hun doth ace say ye an' a tea scene.
Ode the they. Tease. Sea pays Ken a hay own debt row woe 'n' day.
"Zeus key these stem a yeast. Tick gay 'ja' than a teeth, eh. Ali?
Up poet to reap rotary (Ee!) pay. Roar key a 'pee-me-neon.'
Oh the swanky phallus hum at these, Rae. Oh? So they in us?
Oft tone gay tech yawn: 'All how he th' alley seethe the me in.'"
        Oh syph fun new! The raw Po's fin a pack rye necro-neon.
Tease seethe the thar, the need these pre-ammos met a me, though own
        ape pay.
"Cake 'll eat 'em eft. Row us, gay. Ache knee meet the saw. (Hey!) Ye
Eat ye egg. O knee me pro tea Ilion knee name Wesson.
Apse up, you poet. Lease some men off th' all-me-sin nor us they
Mar (nah!) men knowin' feelin'. Y' own are: 'Reef feel loam men allow.'
Zev's men puto (yayy!) the gay a thawin' a teeth, eh, ya Ali?
O poet, to row the knotty oat tail loss, pep Roman honest teen."
        Era gay as thief. Rowin' Arno's they toys. So they, us foes?
On the raven off dusk gotta thee knee, a teen in no piece so.
'Pod,' they yawn. Dinner pear reek a lay, a 'V,' sate oath if Ron.
Ptomaine are up, sorry pro-tea Leon a pone. Neigh 'own doe.'
Hector dip Priam me you país gay. Thee us, Odysseus.
Whorin' men pro tone the aim betrayin' oft a repeat 'Ta.'
Clear ruse sink key neigh. Hulk ear rape pollen nail lone days.
Oh putter us thee, prose Thane. A fee ye hulk k.o. neighin' hoss.
Lie thee reasoned? Oh they seethe. The hair Ross on us, ace cone.

197

Ode the 'they,' tea seep ace Ken Achaians' and Trojans' day.
"Zev potter reed thee thin. May they own kitty stay? May yeast stay?
Oh poet to roast a there, gum it. Tom fought a reason, a thick gay.
Tone those up off thee, men. On thee? Nay, though moan Aïda's see-saw,
He mean the feel o' teat o' gay orc. Key up beast, a yen is they."
       Oh sorry, fawn pollen. They may gas Cory, they a low sector.
Up sorrow own par ya us. They, though, sick (clear) rose. Sore ruse sane.
Eee! Men a pee thee zone ducat a stick (ah!). See, he accost O.
Eee! Pee ire see Poe th' escape peak helot if 'hey' a key toe.
Oft a rogue gum foamy scene o' thee, set at 'tiff hey a call, là.'
Thee, oh Saul, lick sand rose, sell Lenny's pose (sí, sí). Eck! Comb me you
Can knee me thus, men. Pro top Eric knee me scene a thick gay.
Callas, are ye Rae's scene? A peace fear ease Sir Arias.
Theft Aaron off Thor. Reek o' Perry's teeth, Essene? Nay, thee neighin':
'Yolk cause signet eel leak cow.' Nosier Moe say: 'Th' off toe.'
Ump fee the Romey scene valet toke syph us. Are Roy? Loan?
Hulky own oft tarry, peat toss. A cuss mega-taste Steve Aaron day.
Carotid the beef theme Okie neighin' knave teak tone ethic, Ken.
He poor, e'en thee knowin' they'll off us, Kathy pair thinnin' Evan.
Eel late toe th' alky moanin' 'Hoe owe (Ee!) pal o' me.' Feein' a rear? Eee!
Oh stuffed toe's men, a louse sorry. Io send dead Dean in.
       Eee! The Punic otter they know me, Lou, though reek thee, son.
Ass masoned row own gay a 'hey, onus tea!' Hoe owned dough.
Thee knowin' they're comin' 'neath thumb woes, the Kenny sorrow owned us.
Trow was thee, Poe. The moose cake knee me, thus saw 'hey, youse.'
Caring yeast eating the Ahmet tree, toe 'n' knee whore roe.
See yond Deng? He as': 'Ali lea scene caught ye on Day?'
Prose they the lake sand rose pro ye, though lick hose key 'n' unhose.
Gay valet not Rae, though caught a speed the pond does ace scene.
Ooh! They reek! Sink hulk cussin' egg Nam (Pff!) thee they (yecch!) me.
Asp pee th' any craw Thieriot: The 'they've Tehran' or 'neat-o hulk-o'
Ought Rae. Ye these ma' Nell louse sip if f'k summon nose. Thee pottery!
"Zev, Anna those tease sauce they'll map rotor-rose cock Kay or yea!
Thee own Alec sawn, thrown. Gay Emmy sip O'Hare, see the Ma sewn
Off. Rot is heir ye seek. Gay up. Seagull known, non-throw pun-
K. See, know, though cone cock 'll wreck sail. Ken feel a teat top. Pa raw as he."
       Eee! Rock gay ump pep alone. Pro ye, though Lea hose keyin' ain' hoss.

Give a lip rea'. A me thou. Cut asp, pee the pond. Oh say, ye scene.
The ominous pee those seal they fine niece so free moan in hose.
Gay the authoric cuss. Pulley they th' all wearier east toe.
Auntie, creed the par rail lop par. E'en the *ami* say he tone gnaw.
In hose, sew the clean thick gay. Ah love a tokey raw male lain on.
Odd day these, there is some on husk. Sea foes, are ye roilin'?
Blixen, Nana's home in us Cory thus follow Nam fee the rough toe.
Trick, though a gay Tet rock, thaw the 'ought,' reef in ache, Pesach heroes.
Ought Rae? Ye these, though muck sane need, though niece sewer a
                known knave her in
"Zev putter root tea see (Oh? They own?) ol' low oater rose aloes.
Eat tough, a mean tease us, they'll lick sawn throne caulk. Oat eat us.
Knee 'n' the me 'n' he race in a yeek. See fuss sack the me 'n' hose.
Eeech! Thee pal o' me? Fee net toes. See a new. They've alone mean."
        Eek! Gay up Ike's ass. Cory those Slav in neap. Oh, the cease!
Elk aid the beast rips us mate ache knee me thus a 'hey youse.'
On heather mean Pauly kissed us, y *más*! Apple lean neap o' th' earring.
Oh see upon the rail, know. So have stated toe tree folly ease.
Kenny, Kenny, recent deck. Gay as pet oh near rot toke. Key those.
Eee! Me are oak scene, we say 'thee.' Us thick a tear rough row thee tea.
Eee! Ye reek sin, Amanda. Foes see fick, Tom. Many? Oh.
Keeny the tree fall Leia mess pate, oh hear. Reap a he, ye.
Teen men a pithy Rose met. Ache knee me thus a 'hey youse.'
Reap say 'pee, thee, nieces.' Comb Miss on their ear, russet Terry.
Off tarot up zipper, ruse *sec* attack Tom *Mene Mene* known.
In 'hey hulk,' you tone thick. Sir Pox (afro thee tea).
Rhea moll low. Stay, they owe sick a leap, say the rear ripply.
Cod! Thee send th' Alamo! Ever they key Wendy.
Of teeth, of the Lenin call lay, you see a teen, the key honey.
Peer go if heap seal. Lope Perry that royal easy sawin'.
Harry the nectary way annuity knock sail. A vous, ça?
Greed the mean ache. Ya pal lay, ya neigh. Prose ape pen.
Here Ah come, oh. Eee! Eee! Lack o' them money net (ow!) sea.
Ease keen ear ya, call 'em all Easter. The mean feel less gay.
Teemin' ace saw many prose if phone neigh. Thee off roe, thee tea.
"They've wreath a lick sand throe, sick a leak on the nes' they.
Keen nose soy Nth Alamo gay thee note tease seal a hussy.

Calais test teal, von Gay, ye mossy new thick F-face.
On three, Ma Hess amen known. Tone yell 'Thin, Allah whore own they?'
E'er haste thee a whore, Rio Neon league under Kathy's sin."

Horse fat, oat either. Raw thee moan any's teeth a sin arena.
Care Rose sooner, noisy. The Assbery call ya th' earring
'S teeth, the 'Aah.' Thee mare went ducky, oh Muddah mar mayor, own Da.
Thumby send a repeat eye post if a' decked ton o' Ma's. Eee!
"Them money eat. Team met oft, tally le-e-e-eper o' paving.
Eee! Pee may pro tear, rope oleo knave, Naomi noun.
Act sissy! Three ye see me, *honi*. Say 'wrought teen knees.'
Eat tease, teak gay Keith thief feel us. Marrow pone on throw pone.
Ooh naked thee kneein' the own Alex on throne men allow us.
Nicky saw us, Ethel leased earring America, the 'yes, they.'
Two naked thee kneein'. They've road, though. Loaf run you supper rest ease.
Ease supper often you saw they own the poi cackle left Thu.
Me that easy. Seep o' the scene neap o' strip. See a soul limbo!
'Allay ye Perry keen owin' no easier gay,' a' feel lass say.
Ease sock a seal, a hon' piece set 'hey' (oyez!) Thu lean.
Keys said they gone nukey, mean. A mess, Seton, they Kenny ye.
Keen new pour sunny use saw. Le host row Ed. Them mope piss so.
Pa say mo': 'Me Sunday!' 'Ech!' 'Hoe the hay,' 'accrete a theme' (oh?)."

Teen they hello saw many prose, say 'Phone he thee. Aphrodite?'
"Me merit this he, Lee. Me hose, a many same meth you.
Toast the sop (ech!) theorist knee neck. Pag laugh, feel Lisa.
Meso-thumb fought Aaron meaty. Some may (ech!) the all-league raw.
Trunk gay Donna own see the kink cock cone neat annul Lee (yea!)."

Oh? Syph fought Ed? These send the lay, need the us sickie egg ave (ah!).
'V they caught, us Khomeni, Anwar ye define, no?
'See ye pass us that row was lather near heather,' they moan.

Eh? Thought? Alex and three ode, though Ma 'n' Périchole lay condo.
Am feeble, Lee. Many peter, though. O say, Pe'er got trap, own dough.
Eat these seep sorrow phone th' all a moan key o' the eye 'n' echoin'.
Teethe the wrath. If Ron a loose saw feel amid these afro ditty
Under ya, lick son. Three oath ya caught a thick F'er. Oh ça!
In Thukkoth ease, Hellenic curried you say 'oh heel.'
'Ossible lean clean NASA posin' thee, 'n' he pop Emmy, though.
"Eee! Lead the sick pall, lame woes, so fail less oft (oh?), though less they.

On three, the Miss Scrod. Tarot say mos' pro tarot s'pose he seein'.
He-men the preen (yeah) if, hey, Ah rea''y feel Lou men allow.
Seat Dave, ye gay Herr. See gay in hay if fair terror scene, eh?
Ali fee kneein' pro all less air ye feel lone men allowin'.
Ex oft tease Ma Hess Sauce. They in awe, 'n' d'ya own Allah's ego? Yeah.
Pa vest thick kill low, maim me, thick sawn, though men allow.
On TV own Paul lay, moan. Paul lame, easy knee them, a Hess they.
Off wroth they owes me poster (hee!). He puff tooth (ooh!) wreath the Meese."
         Teen the Paris myth these seen *ami*'ve ominous prose say 'pay.'
"Me may ye nail. Appeasing on need they seethe. Theme moan: a neap day.
Kneein' Ming are Menelaos an' Nicky's ensign, Athene.
Keenin', th' Oft-Tease say: 'Go Pa, regard, they easy came in.'
Ally! Thee feel low teat tit wrap you men of knee, then Day.
Oogh! Are pope ought tame? Moth they arose frayin' us some fecal leaps in?
Ooh! Thought to sip proton. Lack o' them mono-sex Sarah Teenies.
Ape lay on our poxes in pond to pour easy in a yes sea.
Knee sew th' ink. Ron nigh Emmy, yin feel. Low tea tick gay of knee.
Oh say own e'en Aram may gay Meg leak kiss seem Eros airy."
         Era gay are hell. Lay host thick, he own a mod thee, pet tacky tease.
         Tome men are entreaties. Sea caught Evan. Ass then lay (hey!) as sin.
Ought Rae yield these, the no-meal loan effete? A theory ache us.
Eep! Weigh saw, three seein' Alex on throne. They oy, they ah.
All Lou tease the not-oat row, Unc. Lead tone tape peak *couronne*.
Thick sail licks on throne tote a reef. Feel low? Men allow.
Human Gar feel a titty (Yecch!) if the known eat is a thee toe.
Ease sewin' Gar's fin, Pa's sin up Ich. That Okie ear ream Melanie.
Tease sea the quai met ape pinnin' knocks on thrown Agamemnon.
"Kick, cleat 'em after West Gay th' Earth on knee, the pee curry
Nicky mend, the feigned net. Ari feel lumen nail. Ow!
He missed the 'are ye in hell?' Lenin kick team moth o' mufti.
Ache, though ticket team mean up a teen namin' e'en teen achin'.
Eat tech gay? Yes 'm. Many see May 10th throw pee, sea-pale eater."
'Oh,' say Fatah, 'Trade these.' Ape pee'd thee, neighin' alley Achaeans.

A Pin's Fee

*

UNA SOLIDA ESPERIENZA D'AVANGUARDIA

1. THINK DEAD

There would be nothing, a dull buzz, a clichéd c/licking off
Of seens, where everybody's neverendissimo sexy movements
Get lost anyway. The

    a)   Spirit of   lling: When the experience
             Matches the wish, it twists
                        the wish elsewhere.

    b)   No account. Useless.
             You too. Everyone.

    c)   unpronounceable! Only a   could say it.
             To think it "really" would intend horrible crimes.

2. NEO-AFTERS FOREVER

'Basically,' you're dead for four to six billion years, then
Alive for about seventy years,
                        then dead again
For four to six billion years, minimum.
          Most of the time, you're dead.

3. FAT BOY UNUSED TO BRAIN DAMAGE

At the Villa d'Angri lived a little knight of music.
"Nothing labeled, nothing lost," he said.

    "Nothing lost, nothing learned."
                                 Loathing lost.

"Nothing learned, nothing spurned." And so he wrote *Parsifal*.

SINCE YOU QUIT THE "Y" AND MOVED AWAY, YOU HAVEN'T SPOKEN TO ME FOR MORE THAN A FEW MINUTES AT A TIME

1. FABLE

Fed *chose*, ~~she~~
    shows
               clean
clean   bed   chose
bed
        house

      The dog.

CREATE IN THE CREATED

Fie, Duke Large Cone

eyes that promise all,

    hand's ~~breadth~~ breath

Dear Erection (Dear Eckstein)

      invite
lewd
      pub licking.

2. SUJET

At 18, before his first attempt at suicide, he said
"Words are inadequate,"   developed a stutter
      built a tower
        so high that his language fell apart.

3. MORALE

~~spequeautaix~~ spectacle

NOW WHEN YOU DO COME OVER TO VISIT
WE DON'T KNOW WHAT TO SAY TO EACH OTHER

1.

bay   bead

a   reef

~~osprey~~ Chicago

scant

2.

*(cost)   too   much.

yr   hunch

wing

~~Ticks~~   unlickly

air   tail.

3.

fleline

abart

ord

fledge (~~fletgh~~)

ALL THESE GROOVES ARE HEAVENS

1. FABLE

exile.   outdoor prison.   who's in America.

I ~~rove~~ it,   but

w
|

~~lypelim~~   divi / lour

balance

swor   ffring

2. SUJET

For that which is dark is dark within us will not die, will not
Dissolve in

tone

(getting along),

heard ~~since~~

cloven world

horror mundi,

~~since~~

eclipsed world.

3. MORALE

Reckt,   clothes   fallen

              life   ~~slipped~~   off
                    fallen

tunes,   two.

                            Sweet   dead
                            ~~Sweat~~ key in ~~chord~~ dore

     ~~reed~~   rore
        redesign   ~~roar~~.

I DON'T KNOW WHY YOU WANT TO THROW ALL OUR YEARS TOGETHER AWAY

1. FABLE

I'm	up	gutted	~~up~~	up
it	there	going	(I)	there
going	to	If	it	out
If	shoot	gutted	to	I
I'm	shoot	Don't	Don't	it.

2. SUJET

field	tap	fate
it	box	fish
pet	bough	tints

3. MORALE

cjateau

DON'T WANT TO BE ANYONE ELSE'S LOVER

1. FABLE

Three places are messie, dream cause.
Ole! Swijo kataij! See me tarot me tie. Y yo portuj ja. KATAIJ!

I DO recognize you, my siter, my broter, whose seekint gives
Hope to th' world

$$\text{nor musit, uh, mucis.}$$
mm, mMusic.   ARE msuic.

2. SUJET

r genies.   able t ink.   milk guil .

  ro-dot   otal   ario   oreknow

          ought   ootsie   a Onan.   ut   all.

suck he   Omar   rring wove   a sure   ope pot   lue cozy.

                    wise in male type   comfy.

Too prick   usin, suck   ul ion's middle Moe   .

3. MORALE

NO to hatred. NO to fists. NO to slimy reasons.

NO to the sneer. NO to rage coupled with power.

NO to the sway of the wicked.

"Uh, O.K."

WE ZONKED HIM INTO BEING WHORLMLESS

1. FABLE

He said he was trying to start in the middle of a sentence
And move in both directions at the same time.

2. SUJET

Noisy the Sick   stre-

                             tching.

" 'I am good, I am good,' say it."   (You are goo.)

         (You are good.)   (You are goog.)

   turth Edda

3. MORALE

Go Climb Into Yourself

                       fokked / ting

Major pin Gap   prain gap

A LOOSE URN GATHERS NO MOTHS. NO MOTHERS. NO MOSSED.

A POEM FOR TRANSLATORS

1.   FABLE

Whee!   A boat

Trap boot

battle

swat

catch trees

pomp walk

2.   SUJET

weld scene knee goad   wi

weld

seld seen   knee

weld seen kne goa(d)   geld wean

3. MORALE

Wheeled swallow

        smoke flower

   plumb take fire!

I FEEL SO ABANDONED BY YOU I'D LIKE TO DIE

1. FABLE

Dares nothing   Like the dominant.
Ooh , yeh the subdominant.   2.
Itz give and a lyiiit I LIKE THE HARMONIC MINOR.

Seep syeep hypnah.   SLEEP   is a mess   messy wyrrd.
HYPNOS is the way the bugs spell it.   Why a P?   YYNOS, mebby.

I LIKE THE FIRST FOUR NOTES OF THE HARMONIC MINOR
AS IT DESCENNDS FFROM TTHEE TTOONNIICC.

WE UZE double letterz to say watt we mean.

2. SUJET

~~One.~~   Neigh Tsitanss.   It's a pa(r)tinir
O*r* now in the azwement of the praod.
Uze a little sex.   Had we forgotten (   ) sez?
NOW IN THE BASEMENT OF THE PRAOD, BUT USEDTO BE ON
THE 1ST FLOOR.
                Doona light.   TING.   MY PEPHELONE BELL
IS NIT.

            (paing.

3. MORALE

I CANT HERE IT.   I do my jobb.
There are many daf people who do thei rjobs, too.
                              (deres trubble!   'm not dif)
Why my vocabulary is so (amall) (small) is: guitar, clap, nonetheless.
You read this, bUTT lready going to bar to find a love buddy.

TO THE HEAD-IN-THE-AIR PAINTER

1. FABLE

The   ink   hulk

      ate   ink

        shadow.

         His farmer's

   self

                  bleeding lay.

2. SUJET

Feed

              back

    tk-tv   pigs

                garb.

3. MORALE

            Buddy & Colleague.

NOBODY WILL REMEMBER US ANYWAY

1.

~~dairy~~ seen

churl seetest siring

piece zoo ~~we're~~ test.
wheat

yrdy

From   dairy test,

churls.   He's cease

tormented.

2.

(not to follow)

Sunned ~~wait~~
rate

Queene.   wair

claps ~~metal~~ motil eyce

played.

3.

~~share~~ shave

         twisted to get ~~the shift~~

    ~~wh~~ tiring to from

      ~~from~~ the iron

    ~~to~~ get share, of Death   'Tis.

DEATH DEATH   DEATH DEATH

DEATH

DEATH DEATH   DEATH DEATH

1.

DEATH DEATH   DEATH DEATH

DEATH DEATH   DEATH DEATH

DEATH DEATH   DEATH DEATH

2.

DEATH DEATH   DEATH DEATH

DEATH DEATH   DEATH DEATH

DEATH DEATH   DEATH DEATH

3.

DEATH DEATH   DEATH DEATH

DEATH DEATH   DEATH DEATH

DEATH DEATH   DEATH DEATH

A NOTE ON THE TEXTS

*

Eclogs. The first and only prior printing is the Ithaca House edition (1973), solicited and edited by David McAleavey, with a cover selected by David Melnick himself: an illuminated page from the 5th-century Vergilius Romanus. Typescripts of portions of the poem from the Ron Silliman archive at UC San Diego and prior magazine publications show negligible differences, which were ignored at Melnick's request. The text here was prepared by Alison Fraser and Benjamin Friedlander, then proofed by Melnick.

PCOET. The first and only prior printing is the G.A.W.K. edition (1975), prepared for publication by Melnick. That edition employed a typewriter font and featured a plain, gray cover with text and printers' ornaments. Portions of the poem appeared separately in magazines, notably in a special issue of *Tottel's* (no. 13, 1975), edited by Ron Silliman. The text here was originally prepared by Jeffrey Jullich and proofed by Melnick for digital publication, again using a typewriter font. With Melnick's approval the font was changed for *Nice* to match the rest of the volume.

Men in Aïda. Book I was first published by Lyn Hejinian in a letter-press edition as Tuumba no. 47 (1983). The first five words of the Greek were printed on the cover and title page in red. Book II was transcribed from Melnick's typescript by Craig Dworkin and published online on Dworkin's *Eclipse* website in 2002. The texts here of Books I, II, and III were prepared by Alison Fraser and Benjamin Friedlander, checked against all available typescripts, then proofed by Melnick. Prior to its appearance in *Nice*, this version of the complete poem was also published by Uitgeverij with facing Greek script and an introduction by Sean Gurd (2014).

A *Pin's Fee*: First published by Jeffrey Jullich on his Logopoeia website in 2002, brought into print by Mark Francis Johnson, Andy Martrich, and Jonathan Gorman as a Hiding Press chapbook in 2019. The text here is based on that of Jullich, reviewed by Melnick when assembled with the other texts in *Nice*. Some adjustments of spacing have been made to fit the constraints of this edition.

ACKNOWLEDGMENTS

*

The editors are grateful to the family and friends of David Melnick who shared their recollections or answered questions about the publication history of Melnick's work. Daniel Melnick and David Greene were especially generous with time; we could not have completed our introduction without their help. We also thank Rae Armantrout, Carla Billitteri, Steve Benson, Marty Cain, Lynda Claassen, Craig Dworkin, Lyn Hejinian, Mark Johnson, James Maynard, David McAleavy, Daniel Nicoletta, John J. W. Plampin, David Pritchard, Andy Robinson, and Aaron Shurin. For assistance in obtaining archival material, we are indebted to the librarians and staff at The Poetry Collection of the University Libraries, University at Buffalo, The State University of New York; Special Collections Research Center, Syracuse University Library, Syracuse University; Special Collections & Archives, UCSD Library, University of California, San Diego; and The Getty Research Institute. At Nightboat, Stephen Motika welcomed this project and was steadfast in his support. Lindsey Boldt and Gia Gonzales guided us through production. We deeply appreciate their care for David Melnick's work and also for the care given this book by Jaye Elizabeth Elijah, Rissa Hochberger, Kit Schluter, and all others behind the scenes who helped make *Nice* possible.

David Melnick was born in Illinois in 1938 and raised in Los Angeles, educated at the University of Chicago (where he studied with Hannah Arendt) and the University of California at Berkeley. Although he spent time in France, Greece, and Spain (whence his mother's ancestors emigrated in 1492), most of his adult life was centered in San Francisco. For an author's note he once wrote, "This poet's politics are left, his sexual orientation gay, his family Jewish. . . . He is short, fat, and resembles Modeste Moussorgsky in face and Gertrude Stein in body type and posture." Melnick was a skilled musician and student of mathematics before turning to poetry. At Berkeley he participated in the Free Speech movement. He later became a key member of G.A.W.K. (the Gay Artists and Writers Kollective). His first two books, *Eclogs* and *Pcoet*, were early inspirations for Language Writing; his third, *Men in Aida*, began in a reading group organized by Robert Duncan; his last, *A Pin's Fee*, was shaped by the AIDS crisis. A singular figure in American poetry, Melnick passed away in 2022, a day before his 84th birthday.

Alison Fraser is Associate Curator of the Poetry Collection at the University at Buffalo and editor of *The Collages of Helen Adam*.

Benjamin Friedlander is a poet teaching at the University of Maine and editor of Robert Creeley's *Selected Poems 1945-2005*.

Jeffrey Jullich is a poet and lives in New York City.

Ron Silliman is the author or editor of 50 books, among them *The Alphabet* (a long poem), the memoir *Under Albany*, and the watershed anthology *In the American Tree* (which includes the work of David Melnick).

NIGHTBOAT BOOKS

Nightboat Books, a nonprofit organization, seeks to develop audiences for writers whose work resists convention and transcends boundaries. We publish books rich with poignancy, intelligence, and risk. Please visit nightboat.org to learn about our titles and how you can support our future publications.

The following individuals have supported the publication of this book. We thank them for their generosity and commitment to the mission of Nightboat Books:

Kazim Ali • Anonymous (8) • Mary Armantrout • Jean C. Ballantyne • Thomas Ballantyne • Bill Bruns • John Cappetta • V. Shannon Clyne • Ulla Dydo Charitable Fund • Photios Giovanis • Amanda Greenberger • Vandana Khanna • Isaac Klausner • Shari Leinwand • Anne Marie Macari • Elizabeth Madans • Martha Melvoin • Caren Motika • Elizabeth Motika • The Leslie Scalapino - O Books Fund • Robin Shanus • Thomas Shardlow • Rebecca Shea • Ira Silverberg • Benjamin Taylor • David Wall • Jerrie Whitfield & Richard Motika • Arden Wohl • Issam Zineh

This book is made possible, in part, by grants from the New York City Department of Cultural Affairs in partnership with the City Council, the New York State Council on the Arts Literature Program, and the Topanga Fund, which is dedicated to promoting the arts and literature of California.